A JOHN CATT PUBLICATION

Emma Turner, David Goodwin & Oliver Caviglioli

ANNIE MURPHY PAUL'S

THE EXTENDED MIND
IN ACTION

WM

IN ACTION SERIES

EDITOR
TOM SHERRINGTON

DESIGNED & ILLUSTRATED BY ORGANISE IDEAS

A WALKTHRUs PRODUCTION

First Published 2022

by John Catt Educational Ltd,
15 Riduna Park, Station Road,
Melton, Woodbridge IP12 1QT

Tel: +44 (0) 1394 389850
Email: enquiries@johncatt.com
Website: www.johncatt.com

ISBN: 978 1 915261 00 7

Set and designed by John Catt Educational Limited

EMMA TURNER

For Emma, the ideas within this book enhance, underpin and amplify what we know about best practice in primary education. The book serves to articulate the research base, explaining how the cognitive is enhanced by movement, working with others and representing thinking – all of which are found in the best primary classrooms.

DAVID GOODWIN

For David, this book feels like a natural extension of his previous book *Organise Ideas*, co-authored with Oliver. While working on OI, it became clear to David that the concept of the extended mind – when placed alongside established learning models – might advance our understanding of how learning happens.

OLIVER CAVIGLIOLI

Throughout his time in special education, Oliver witnessed the poor fit of policies designed for other sectors. The notions and evidence of *The Extended Mind* give teachers a framework to articulate the complexity of their practice. After 40 years in education, Oliver is honoured to acknowledge the brilliance of everyday teaching.

CONTENTS

SITUATED
COGNITIVE
LOOP

EMBODIED
COGNITIVE
LOOP

DISTRIBUTED
COGNITIVE
LOOP

WM

MEMORISED
COGNITIVE
LOOP

SERIES FOREWORD

TOM SHERRINGTON

The idea for the *In Action* series was developed by John Catt's *Teaching WalkThrus* team after we saw how popular our *Rosenshine's Principles in Action* booklets proved to be. We realised that the same approach might support teachers to access the ideas of a range of researchers, cognitive scientists and educators. A constant challenge that we wrestle with in the world of teaching and education research is the significant distance between the formulation of a set of concepts and conclusions that might be useful to teachers and the moment when a teacher uses those ideas to teach their students in a more effective manner, thereby succeeding in securing deeper or richer learning. Sometimes so much meaning is lost along that journey, through all the communication barriers that line the road, that the implementation of the idea bears no relation to the concept its originator had in mind. Sometimes it's more powerful to hear from a teacher about how they implemented an idea than it is to read about the idea from a researcher or cognitive scientist directly – because they reduce that distance; they push some of those barriers aside.

In our *In Action* series, the authors and their collaborative partners are mainly teachers or school leaders close to the action in classrooms in real schools. Their strategies for translating their subject's work into practice bring fresh energy to a powerful set of original ideas in such a way that we're confident will support teachers with their professional learning and, ultimately, their classroom practice. In doing so they are also paying their respects to the original researchers and their work.

In education, as in so many walks of life, we are standing on the shoulders of giants. We believe that our selection of featured researchers and papers represents some of the most important work done in the field of education in recent times.

In this book, Oliver, David and Emma have, to some extent, broken the series mould, adapting the *In Action* concept to explore Annie Murphy Paul's work on *The Extended Mind* in an exploratory fashion, testing out how it applies in various contexts, widening the view of learning captured within more accepted memory models. It's a superb addition to the range of ideas represented in the series.

Finally, in producing this series, we would like to acknowledge the significant influence of the researchED movement run by Tom Bennett that started in 2013. I was present at the first conference and, having seen the movement grow from strength over the intervening years, I feel that many of us, including several *In Action* authors, owe a significant debt of gratitude to researchED for providing the forum where teachers' and researchers' ideas and perspectives can be shared. We are delighted, therefore, to be contributing a share of the royalties to researchED to support them in their on-going non-profit work.

FOREWORD

Annie Murphy Paul, award-winning science writer and author of The Extended Mind.

ANNIE MURPHY PAUL

As I've learned over the course of my career, an author doesn't know the readership a book will find until the book is out there in the world. To my delight, the most enthusiastic readership for my recent book, *The Extended Mind*, has been teachers and school leaders. In retrospect, this makes perfect sense. Educators spend their lives thinking about how to create contexts in which students will learn and think best, and that's really what my book is about.

Although I borrowed the theory of the extended mind from the philosophers Andy Clark and David Chalmers, the idea is no pie-in-the-sky ivory-tower abstraction. To the contrary, it is an intensely practical and useful way of thinking about how our minds work. Rather than being sealed inside the skull, Clark and Chalmers argue, the mind extends into the world: into our bodies, into our physical surroundings, into our relationships with other people, and into our tools and technologies. What this means for teaching and learning is that we do not only need to cultivate the brain; we need to cultivate the brain's capacity to extend itself with all the resources at hand.

Since *The Extended Mind* was published, I have heard from educators that the book gave them a theoretical framework, and scientific backing, for approaches and techniques they were already employing in the classroom. I think this is because the theory of the extended mind is deeply rooted in our nature as human beings: as embodied creatures, embedded in physical space, profoundly connected to others and crucially assisted by our tools. I am pleased beyond measure that Emma Turner, David Goodwin, and Oliver Caviglioli – three thinkers I greatly admire – have brought the ideas in *The Extended Mind* even closer to the world of students and teachers.

FOREWORD

Martha Alibali is a Vilas Distinguished Achievement Professor of Psychology and Educational Psychology at the University of Wisconsin-Madison

**MARTHA
ALIBALI**

'The feet are the wheels of the mind', a wise friend once told me, explaining why he liked to walk to work. Moving our bodies can help us think. This idea resonated with me, because my own research is on how children gesture as they learn mathematics. But, as Annie Murphy Paul argues in *The Extended Mind*, movement is not the only thing that gives the mind *wheels*. Well-designed spaces, time in nature, representational tools, and interactions with others can also help people solve problems, generate new ideas, and learn concepts and skills.

Of course, thinking involves the brain, but Murphy Paul makes a compelling case that thinking is not *brainbound*. She marshals research from many fields – including psychology and education, but also anthropology, business, communication studies, theatre, and medicine – to highlight the multifaceted roles of bodies, spaces, and social interaction in thinking. People think using bodies that feel and move, in natural and physical spaces that are filled with objects and cultural tools, and in social and community settings that provide opportunities to distribute cognitive labour and to imitate and build on others' ideas.

These insights about how the mind is extended in bodies, spaces, and social settings hold important lessons for educational practice. In this book, Turner, Goodwin and Caviglioli distil key insights from the large body of evidence that Murphy Paul reviews. They consider the implications of this broader perspective on the mind for the design of learning environments and learning activities. They also bring teachers' voices and ideas into the discussion, spotlighting the myriad and creative ways in which teachers use movement, space, and social interaction to foster student engagement and to promote learning. By sharing both theoretical ideas and practical recommendations, this book will inspire readers to generate new ways to give wheels to learners' minds.

MEL AINSCOW CBE
Emeritus Professor of Education, University of Manchester

The global priority for education systems is to address the challenge of inclusion and equity. A guide published by UNESCO in 2017 sums up this theme as follows: 'Every learner matters and matters equally.'

The implication is that those of us involved in education have to value all our students as individuals. In this respect, learner differences within our classrooms take on a new role. Rather than presenting us with problems to be fixed – or even taken away – the varied ways in which individuals learn can provide a stimulus for our continuing professional learning.

The ideas in this book offer much food for thought in relation to this crucial agenda. In particular, they encourage us to think about the various ways in which learning can take place. They do this through messages that are largely theoretical. This reminds me of the advice of one of the modern pioneers of social, organisational, and applied psychology, Kurt Lewin, who argued, 'There is nothing so practical as a good theory.'

DARREN HANKEY
Principal, Hartlepool FE College

In recent years, cognition has been a dominant narrative in the field of education. Much of this is useful for educators to gain a greater understanding of learning, memory and the human cognitive architecture. This book builds on this by examining how other external factors – gestures, the environment and groups – can aid the learning process. For practitioners who operate in vocational and technical education, this will be invaluable. Think of those who deliver construction, civil engineering and sports programmes, to name but a few, whose environment is a key learning resource. In addition, those who deliver health and social care and early years programmes instil the use of gestures and team work as a key part of this provision. Further education colleges have a long and well-established track record providing high-quality education and training for learners with SEND and the principles in this book will be invaluable for the practitioners working in this important space.

DAME ALISON PEACOCK
CEO, Chartered College of Teaching

These spreads provide detailed evidenced examples of the way in which mind and body are intertwined. Those of us who have spent time educating very young children will know how their very act of explaining is inevitably accompanied by gesture. Impact of new stimuli or a different environment shows itself clearly through physical response in the young learner. The notion of learning being optimal when effort is being made to keep the body still is debunked.

The physical act of writing or drawing as a means of capturing thought, thereby reducing cognitive load and extending the mind, is so obvious once stated. As indeed is the process of learning digitally when passive listening is replaced by dialogic interaction.

There is much here to excite teachers and to inspire effective learning in both formal and informal situations and much to reaffirm early years methodology.

SAM STRICKLAND
Principal of a large all-through school, author, speaker and conference organiser

As part of your classroom practice or school improvement journey you have behaviour systems in place, clear routines for learning, watertight deliberate practice actioned and a clear curricular approach. So surely it is a case of job done? *The Extended Mind* invites you to think about the all-important 'what next?' This read both informs and reaffirms our collective understanding of cognitive science. It offers the reader a clear insight into approaches to both human cognitive architecture and cognition in general.

There is a clever interplay between theory, leading voices in the field of cognitive science and, most importantly of all, a clear and simple translation as to how this can form part of the enacted curriculum. If you want a snappy read that will allow you to really consider cognition then this is it.

FOUR
COGNITIONS

SITUATED
COGNITIVE
LOOP

EMBODIED
COGNITIVE
LOOP

DISTRIBUTED
COGNITIVE
LOOP

MEMORISED
COGNITIVE
LOOP

WHY THIS BOOK?

In an evidence-informed world, The Extended Mind helps address gaps in our understanding of cognition.

Enriching our view of the learning process

The Extended Mind by award-winning science writer, Annie Murphy Paul, is making waves. While not a straight education book, it's entirely focused on how we think and learn. Chock-full of evidence, it identifies, integrates and illustrates the multimodal nature of cognition.

It is useful to see it as sitting alongside Dan Willingham's well-known and established model of memory. In this light, the still-developing science of cognition offers teachers opportunities to see which of the ideas might be useful in their classrooms. And how they contribute to a more rounded understanding of the learning process. Some may see even it as echoing Allan Paivio's Dual Coding Theory with its verbal and non-verbal composite.

Allan Paivio

MENTAL REPRESENTATIONS HAVE THEIR DEVELOPMENTAL ORIGIN IN PERCEPTUAL, MOTOR AND AFFECTIVE EXPERIENCE.

Addressing your concerns

Teachers are rightly tired of celebrities, business people and politicians telling them how to teach. There's no other profession that is subject to such unqualified advice. So to assuage such concerns, here are recommendations from two of our most respected writers. Given the rigour of their thinking, these reviews should trigger your curiosity.

Dan Willingham

The Extended Mind is not just a fascinating read, firmly grounded in science – it will help you, and your students and your children, to think better.

BOOK REVIEW ON AMAZON.COM

Doug Lemov

It will take you on a journey to a hundred deeper applications of the emerging science that suggests that the mind thinks within, with and through the body.

BOOK REVIEW ON AMAZON.COM

Science

With ~~God~~ on our side.

Bob Dylan, 1964

Follow the science

Rather like in Bob Dylan's famous protest song, arguments in today's educational scene are won by more secure and frequent references to *the science*. Holding a position counter to the quoted science is an admission of being a contemporary flat-earther.

All the more reason, then, to be clear and current on what the science is around all aspects of learning. This book introduces readers to a theory and a new collection of studies that promise to resonate with aspects of practice.

SEE **SPREAD 05 & 07**
FOR UPDATES ON
COGNITIVE SCIENCE &
COGNITIVE LOAD
THEORY

Intentions of this In Action book

INFORM & UPDATE	Understand why cognitive psychology got an upgrade to cognitive science, and what key belief is shared by the disciplines within that domain.
REVIEW & EXEMPLIFY	A tour of three cognitions, hitherto unlabelled, and their relationship to the brain within cognitive loops. And to show examples when applied.
VALIDATE & INTEGRATE	The naming of all aspects of learning to establish a shared lexicon – showing how cognitive loops can serve ulterior mental processes.
SPARK & FERMENT	Stimulate reading Murphy Paul's book and fermenting debate to reveal the multilayered practice of many sectors in education.

CRITIQUE AND CONTROVERSY

New ways of looking at the familiar can cast light on the familiar. But it's often not an easy ride to get there.

Boundary conditions

As fulsome as the hundreds of research papers referenced in the book are, very few come directly from classrooms. And as context – technically: boundary conditions – is critical in assessing the relevance of any piece of evidence, this places the ideas in the book, as far as education is concerned, as work in progress.

In itself, this doesn't invalidate the use of evidence from other, non-educational sources. Indeed, we note that several of today's leading educational authors make reference to the developing discipline of behavioural economics as well as to self-help and productivity authors.

The learning styles question

As expected, the notion of embodied cognition has received concerned responses about the return of learning styles. On the surface – that is to say without either a knowledge of cognitive psychology, or familiarity with the philosophical and empirical basis of the extended mind – there are superficial similarities. But a cursory read should dispel such a misconception.

Annie Murphy Paul

ALL LEARNERS BENEFIT WHEN INFORMATION IS PUT FORTH IN DIVERSE WAYS THAT ENGAGE A MULTITUDE OF THE SENSES.

At a slightly deeper level, some might still have concerns that most teachers do not have such knowledge. In which case, their arguments run, they can't be trusted not to end up recreating the selfsame mistakes of learning styles of earlier times and, again, impeding the learning of students.

But for a profession committed to a knowledge-rich curriculum and an evidence-informed pedagogy, such withholding of knowledge is untenable. We note criticisms that some schools have used knowledge organisers – a method of identifying key elements in a unit of study – as a misconceived substitute for a knowledge-rich curriculum. Even if true, that is no reason to suppress their use.

Similarly so with the ideas of the extended mind. The solution, as ever, is education. This book encourages teachers to read more about the multilayered nature of cognition and the loops within it.

CHAPTER
FOUR COGNITIONS

SPREADS
01 WHY THIS BOOK? | **02 CRITIQUE & CONTROVERSY** | 03 PHILOSOPHICAL ORIGINS |
04 METAPHORS | 05 COGNITIVE SCIENCE | 06 EVOLUTIONARY PSYCHOLOGY |
07 COGNITIVE LOAD THEORY | 08 INFOGRAPHIC SUMMARY

Keeping the end in mind

Once the issue of learning styles is rightly relegated to circus sideshow status, the serious business begins of how to exploit the potential of the extended mind.

Above all, it's critical to frame such endeavours as serving the end goal of intellectual progress. The established and shared vocabulary should aid a rigorous monitoring of how the ideas in the book are marshalled for this purpose. At no point is the centrality of the working/long-term memory cognitive loop questioned. It remains where the intellect functions but also, we now know, how it is enriched and informed by interactions with the body, the world, its tools, and other people.

Alison Abbott

BUT LET'S NOT EXAGGERATE: IT'S THE BRAIN, AND NOT THE BODY, THAT DOES THE ACTUAL THINKING.

The power of explanation

What the framework offers is a solution to the sense that a few sectors in education feel misunderstood and alienated from an entirely exam-focused secondary agenda.

Why has this situation occurred you may ask? We think it is due to the lack of a satisfactory intellectual framework through which special, early years and FE professionals can articulate their expertise in relation to the learning needs of their contexts. Explanations using terms like 'holistic' merely trigger cynical taunts of fuzzy, New Age magical thinking. What has been lacking thus far is an evidence-informed foundation based on cognitive science.

The power of the everyday

We think that when you see the teachers' case stories from all sectors, you will be disappointed by their ordinariness. You may find them inspirational and useful in many respects – but none are magical or New Age. They are quotidian, they are responsible, they are effective.

This book is no manifesto for a revolution or a demand for policy change. It is a recognition of what is happening in our classrooms: multiplying points of access to the curriculum and supporting all learners to learn their best.

PHILOSOPHICAL ORIGINS
Philosophy has changed the course of several disciplines within the umbrella term cognitive science.

George Lakoff & Mark Johnson

DESCARTES' VIEW IS NOT A QUAINT SEVENTEENTH CENTURY ODDITY OF MERE HISTORICAL INTEREST. IT IS VERY MUCH WITH US TODAY.

Our ongoing delusion

French philosopher, René Descartes, has a lot to answer for. His view that the mind is divorced from the body – indeed is of a completely different nature – has persisted for over 300 years. And for over a hundred years has been debunked by fellow philosophers. Yet it persists.

It resonates so strongly with common sense that, for most people, it remains their own unexamined schema. Like a superstition, however, it persists by not being conscious. In this sense, it's as if a superstition remains a superstition when it isn't. That's to say, when brought out into the open and analysed, it no longer operates as a superstition in quite the same pernicious way.

A famously beguiling conversation

Richard Feynman

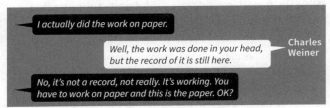

I actually did the work on paper.

Well, the work was done in your head, but the record of it is still here.

Charles Weiner

No, it's not a record, not really. It's working. You have to work on paper and this is the paper. OK?

The notion of the mind extending into the world is illustrated by this conversation between physicist Richard Feynman and historian Charles Weiner. Working together on a project, Feynman produced a paper of their work. This brief exchange they had revealed their different ideas about the nature and workings of the mind.

The breakthrough paper

In 1998, philosophy professors Andy Clark and David Chalmers wrote a paper titled *The Extended Mind*. It started with the arresting question quoted to the left. In answering their own question, they were to alter the course of the disciplines contained within the umbrella of cognitive science. They have rigorously defended the inevitable reactions against their major proposition that the mind properly understood is, indeed, extended.

Andy Clark & David Chalmers

WHERE DOES THE MIND STOP AND THE REST OF THE WORLD BEGIN?

The Extended Mind in action

Over the subsequent 20 years, Andy Clark has given us a number of different examples that illustrate the intimate relationship our brains have with our bodies, objects, the world and other people. Here are just some of them.

https://youtu.be/
hanv8y_wYEQ

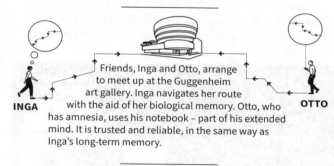

Friends, Inga and Otto, arrange to meet up at the Guggenheim art gallery. Inga navigates her route with the aid of her biological memory. Otto, who has amnesia, uses his notebook – part of his extended mind. It is trusted and reliable, in the same way as Inga's long-term memory.

INGA　　　　　　　　**OTTO**

Andy Clark

COGNITION LEAKS OUT INTO THE BODY AND THE WORLD.

 When Eva, suffering from dementia, was taken from her home with its familiarity, her competence rapidly plummeted. 'It's a little bit like giving someone a bit of brain damage during their sleep,' explains Clark.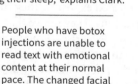

 People who have botox injections are unable to read text with emotional content at their normal pace. The changed facial state slows down their cognitive understanding.

Stephen Jay Gould

NATURE ALSO INCLUDES CONTINUA THAT CANNOT BE NEATLY PARCELED INTO TWO PILES OF UNAMBIGUOUS YESSES AND NOES.

Persuaded?

At this point in the book, your answer isn't important. Indeed, it can be a hindrance. This is not a dichotomy: there is no definite 'Yes' or 'No'. As Stephen Jay Gould reminds us, continua may more accurately represent nature than distinct categories. But, dear reader, we do expect you to have had your assumptions about cognition ruffled somewhat. Read on.

METAPHORS

Our thinking is largely metaphoric, based on what we learned about the world when we were mere toddlers.

George Lakoff

THE SCIENCE IS CLEAR. METAPHORICAL THOUGHT IS NORMAL.

The book that started it all

In 1980, cognitive linguist George Lakoff and philosopher Mark Johnson published a book titled *Metaphors We Live By*. In it, they revealed the hitherto unnoticed phenomenon of how the majority of our thinking is enabled by the use of metaphors. Not literary flourishes but the everyday use of prepositions, for example, to denote relationships between abstract ideas. Indeed, treating ideas as if they were objects that we manipulate.

More is up

A prelinguistic image schema's development into adult conceptual metaphor. And all without our awareness.

| PRELINGUISTIC IMAGE SCHEMA | CHILD'S LINGUISTIC EXPRESSION | *INVISIBLE* ADULT METAPHOR |

The Dow Jones is up by...

1 2 3 4 5

5 is higher than 3

BREAKING NEWS

Jean Mandler

IMAGE SCHEMAS ARE THE FIRST CONCEPTUAL STRUCTURES.

Image schemas

As soon as they can, babies, then toddlers, experiment with the world in an attempt to understand how it works. Gradually, with repeated exposure, they come to realise some invariable patterns. They notice that when glasses are filled with liquids, the level rises. Equally, they notice the same phenomenon in building a pile of toy bricks: the more bricks, the higher the pile. Without any language to capture this understanding, toddlers nonetheless absorb these *image schemas* (their technical term) and, later, find linguistic expressions for them.

SEE **ORGANISE IDEAS, P.24**: HOW METAPHORS ARE UNKNOWINGLY EMBEDDED INTO OUR EVERYDAY SPEAKING

Metaphors and abstract thinking

With pen and paper, listen carefully to any TED Talk on YouTube. Note down any word or phrase that is not literal. For example, the phrase *grasp an idea* is metaphorical. Ideas, of course, can't actually be grasped. Complete the activity then mull over what you've discovered: abstract thinking is a near impossibility without metaphor.

Spatial metaphors

While there are innumerable metaphors, the most relevant to abstract thinking are the spatial ones. The container image schema is central to most of our intellectual endeavours. Indeed Aristotle's system of logic is entirely based on it. Our abstract thinking, then, is embodied, rooted in the physical.

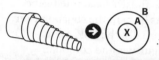

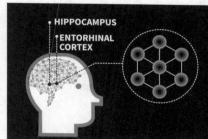

George Lakoff

SPATIAL-RELATIONS ARE AT THE HEART OF OUR CONCEPTUAL SYSTEM.

Grid cells

Cognitive scientists, May-Britt and Edvard Moser, won a Nobel prize for identifying the grid cells in our brains that organise both our sense of place and, very tellingly, our ideas. Links with spatial metaphors are firmly grounded.

The birth of embodied cognition

Lakoff and Johnson's book *Metaphors We Live By* can, in retrospect, be understood to have been the birth of a new discipline within cognitive science: embodied cognition. And as its philosophical implications were so significant – our thinking is entirely embodied – it has also considerably influenced the whole of cognitive science. This triggers a reappraisal of cognition, enriched by the notion of a loop in which information passes from body to brain and back.

Barbara Tversky

THE SAME NEURAL FOUNDATION THAT SERVES SPATIAL THOUGHT SERVES ABSTRACT THOUGHT.

From image schema to the language of business

This conceptual metaphor is the very basis of our notions of progress. We would be *lost* without it.

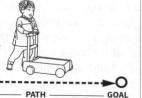

Let's look at the progress towards your annual targets ...

SOURCE ——— PATH ——— GOAL

COGNITIVE SCIENCE
Cognitive psychology is continually influenced by its membership of this multidisciplinary scientific community.

George Miller

A.R. LURIA WAS ONE OF THE FIRST TO SEE THE BRAIN AND MIND AS A WHOLE.

The birth of cognitive science
In George Miller's 2003 personal history of cognitive science, he describes the end of behaviourist psychology in the late 1950s and the consequent focus on internal cognitive processes. At the time, this was also happening in disciplines such as linguistics and artificial intelligence. So by 1960 cognitive science was born in the collaboration between different disciplines. Initially, the links were mostly between psychology, linguistics and computer science (artificial intelligence). But by the time of this paper, Miller attests to substantial bodies of work between all collaborative configurations.

In the diagram Miller used in the paper, you will see no direct link between philosophy and the other disciplines. You will note, however, that it sits above them all, marking its continual and profound influence.

SEE **SPREAD 03** AND OPPOSITE, TO KNOW A LITTLE OF HOW PHILOSOPHY SHAPES OTHER DISCIPLINES

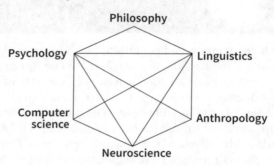

SOURCE: MILLER, G. A., THE COGNITIVE REVOLUTION: A HISTORICAL PERSPECTIVE, 2003.

Early developments
After the 'hollow organism' (nothing going on inside) of behaviourism, the opposite notion took hold: the brain computing. Thus, the ever popular computer metaphor. Indeed, this metaphor was part and parcel of the new identity of cognitive science. Now, human minds were busy computing symbolic representations of the outside world. Such algorithmic formulations became the hallmark of artificial intelligence (computer science).

CHAPTER
FOUR COGNITIONS

SPREADS
01 WHY THIS BOOK? | 02 CRITIQUE & CONTROVERSY | 03 PHILOSOPHICAL ORIGINS |
04 METAPHORS | **05 COGNITIVE SCIENCE** | 06 EVOLUTIONARY PSYCHOLOGY |
07 COGNITIVE LOAD THEORY | 08 INFOGRAPHIC SUMMARY

**FOUR
COGNITIONS**

CHAPTER

1

A new ecological perspective

Interestingly, the modern metaphor of the computer saw a
return of René Descartes to debates – did he ever go away?
Then there was a gradual turning away from his argument
about the complete divorce of mind and body. Escape from
the deluded Cartesian model spelled freedom and new
avenues of research for many.

One man who helped turn psychologists' minds in different
directions was philosopher, Martin Heidegger. With his
phenomenological and ontological approach, the notion of
Dasein – 'being-in-the-world' – captured imaginations. It
no longer seemed valid, or intellectually mature, to continue
pretending to be so objective.

James Gibson, the psychologist, also helped change
perspectives with his shout for a more ecological approach.
That entailed considering the context – the environment
– as being part of the subject. As such, it recognised the
Heideggerian notion of 'being-in-the-world' and not
unattached from it, as the previous cognitivist computer
metaphor assumed. His notion of affordances made
possible an examination of how the environment triggered
psychological responses. Things were changing.

The rebranding of cognitive psychology

Having retitled itself a science, cognitive psychology was
now firmly part of a network of disciplines that were
profoundly influenced by these new turns in philosophy and
accepted the challenges of addressing these more nuanced
and complex phenomena.

Cognitive load theory listened

John Sweller and global colleagues responded, as members
of this science community, to these significant changes.
Also influenced by evolutionary psychology, they started
tackling the effect that the body, the environment and other
people had on one's ability to think effectively within the
limits of working memory.

René Descartes

*THERE IS A GREAT
DIFFERENCE BETWEEN
MIND AND BODY.*

Martin Heidegger

*WE DO NOT 'HAVE'
A BODY; RATHER,
WE 'ARE' BODILY.*

James Gibson

*THE VERB TO AFFORD
IS FOUND IN THE
DICTIONARY, BUT THE
NOUN AFFORDANCE IS
NOT. I HAVE MADE IT UP.*

EVOLUTIONARY PSYCHOLOGY

Geary tells us how critical working memory capacity is to successful learning – and Donald, how to increase it.

Steven Pinker

THE ORIGIN OF MIND IS INVALUABLE … AS A ROAD MAP FOR THE SPRAWLING TERRITORY COVERED BY MODERN PSYCHOLOGY AND NEIGHBOURING SCIENCES.

The Origin of Mind

Published in 2005, David Geary's book of evolutionary psychology has become an increasingly significant framework used to explain the errors of past policies and justify current ones. For educators, its main distinction is between biologically primary and secondary knowledge.

Biologically primary knowledge

This category of knowledge is learned but cannot (easily) be taught. It is learned so readily because our survival depends on it – well it certainly did until very recently. We needed to cooperate with others, success in which depends on what is termed folk psychology. Similarly so with knowledge of plants (folk biology) and objects (folk physics). This knowledge enabled prediction that, in turn, boosted chances of survival.

MANY OF THE WILDER EXPERIMENTS OF PROGRESSIVE EDUCATION WERE DUE TO A FAILURE TO DISTINGUISH THESE TWO DIFFERENT LEARNING PROCESSES

Biologically secondary knowledge

By contrast – and it is a stark contrast – biologically secondary knowledge is learned only if it is taught. And only very recently in our evolutionary span has that occurred in special environments – schools. This type of formal learning involves a great deal of attention and effort, unlike the natural and often unconscious processes of primary learning.

The significance of working memory

David Geary

> *Working memory capacity is one of the primary, if not the primary, cognitive competency underlying fluid intelligence.*

GEARY, D. C., THE ORIGIN OF MIND, 2005

With biologically secondary learning, working memory competency is key, through being able to make rapid connections between long-term memory and working memory processing. You will soon read how other cognitive loops can enlarge working memory capacity.

CHAPTER
FOUR COGNITIONS

SPREADS
01 WHY THIS BOOK? | 02 CRITIQUE & CONTROVERSY | 03 PHILOSOPHICAL ORIGINS |
04 METAPHORS | 05 COGNITIVE SCIENCE | **06 EVOLUTIONARY PSYCHOLOGY** |
07 COGNITIVE LOAD THEORY | 08 INFOGRAPHIC SUMMARY

Origins of the Modern Mind

In his celebrated book, Merlin Donald calls upon his knowledge of cognitive science, neuroanthropology and cognitive neuroscience. Drawing upon these disciplines, he outlines three radical transitions that shaped cognitive and cultural evolution.

When considering the enormous changes in Donald's schema, we should remember that… 'each cognitive adaptation in human evolutionary history has been retained as a fully functional vestige.' Correspondingly, we see many instances of mimetic behaviour in some aspects of learning. We can now understand such aspects of cognition as being embodied, situated and distributed.

Allan Paivio

THE GUIDING THEORETICAL ASSUMPTION IS THAT INTERNAL (MENTAL) REPRESENTATIONS HAVE THEIR DEVELOPMENTAL ORIGIN IN PERCEPTUAL, MOTOR, AND AFFECTIVE EXPERIENCE.

The Mimetic transition		• Early human • Representational acts • Conscious, self-initiated • Public communication
The Mythic transition		• Gestures • Language • Reconstruct the past • Start of symbolism
The Theoretic transition		• External storage of info • External memory field • Iteration & reflection • Public dialectic

GO TO **SPREADS 23 & 25** FOR MORE ABOUT IMITATION & MODELLING

READ MORE ABOUT GESTURES ON **SPREADS 10, 11, 12 & 15**

The affordances of externalising your ideas are many. Transient information is avoided and embodied cognition is triggered.

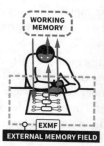

WORKING MEMORY

EXMF
EXTERNAL MEMORY FIELD

External memory … is the exact external analog of internal, or biological, memory.

Merlin Donald

COGNITIVE LOAD THEORY

Through evolutionary psychology, cognitive load theory has included many elements of the extended mind.

Changes in cognitive load theory

Over the past decade, cognitive load theory has developed in ways consistent with the other disciplines of cognitive science and cognitive psychology itself. Significantly so.

CHECK OUT THE OMISSIONS IN RECENT PUBLICATIONS ON CLT

And yet these changes – very strangely – aren't being heralded by followers of the theory. You could be excused for thinking they were being avoided, even *ghosted*.

So what are these changes, and how do they relate to the arguments of the extended mind? We'll reveal them, cognition by cognition, with quotes from a number of eminent researchers behind these developments.

Embodied cognition

Fred Paas

> *Gestures can support WM processing by temporarily off-loading WM resources normally devoted to internal maintenance of information, with the gesture physically maintaining the info.*

PAAS, F. & SWELLER, J., 2012

The title of the paper from which the above quote is taken is very revealing: AN EVOLUTIONARY UPGRADE OF COGNITIVE LOAD THEORY: USING THE HUMAN MOTOR SYSTEM AND COLLABORATION TO SUPPORT THE LEARNING OF COMPLEX COGNITIVE TASKS.

SEE **SPREAD 09** TO READ MORE ABOUT EMBODIED COGNITION

Geary's evolutionary psychology thesis of biologically primary and secondary knowledge is used to explain the benefits of gesture in solving geometry problems. By using their fingers to trace the angles of figures presented, the students outperformed a comparative group who did not use tracing.

GO TO **SPREAD 06** TO LEARN ABOUT GEARY'S BIOLOGICALLY PRIMARY LEARNING

Gestures have no working memory cost yet they store information (here, about the angles of the shapes). The students' working memory capacity was not affected by this and, as a result, could be entirely devoted to other computational tasks. Or, in different terms, embodied cognition gave a hand to memorised cognition. For free.

CHAPTER
FOUR COGNITIONS

SPREADS
01 WHY THIS BOOK? | 02 CRITIQUE & CONTROVERSY | 03 PHILOSOPHICAL ORIGINS |
04 METAPHORS | 05 COGNITIVE SCIENCE |06 EVOLUTIONARY PSYCHOLOGY |
07 COGNITIVE LOAD THEORY | 08 INFOGRAPHIC SUMMARY

Situated cognition

> *The physical learning environment is considered as a distinct causal factor of cognitive load by redefining the term 'environment'.*

CHOI, H.H., van MERRIENBOER, J. & PAAS, F., 2014

Jeroen van
Merriënboer

This was the first attempt to investigate the effect of the environment on cognitive load, both theoretically and empirically. The result was a rewriting of parts of the original cognitive load theory where now: 'the environment is considered a distinct causal factor that can interact with learner characteristics, learning-task characteristics'.

SEE **SPREAD 16** TO
READ MORE ABOUT
SITUATED COGNITION

Distributed cognition

> *The collective working memory concept has an important focus on the learning of individuals in the group.*

KIRSCHNER, P., SWELLER J., KIRSCHNER,
F. & ZAMBRANO, J., 2018

Paul Kirschner

Others make a difference to our thinking and learning. They do this in a number of ways: being a soundboard for our ideas, providing feedback, contributing ideas and holding information in group working memory.

SEE **SPREAD 23** TO
READ MORE ABOUT
DISTRIBUTED
COGNITION

On this last point much depends on the nature of the task in relation to the students' prior knowledge. As Femke Kirschner points out, the critical nature of the contents' complexity determines the effectiveness of group work.

> *Quite simply, when learning material is low in complexity, individual learning is superior. However, when learning complex information, collaborative learning is more effective than individual learning.*

Femke Kirschner

KIRSCHNER, F., PAAS, F. & KIRSCHNER P., 2018

INFOGRAPHIC SUMMARY

When different disciplines and studies are connected, their significance and our understanding is greatly enhanced.

Annie Murphy Paul

THE EXTENDED MIND

MEMORISED COGNITIVE LOOP

The circuitry of information from working memory to long-term memory and back.

EMBODIED COGNITIVE LOOP

The cognitive loop from body, its movements and feelings to working memory.

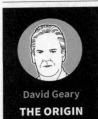

Merlin Donald

ORIGINS OF THE MODERN MIND

EPISODIC ERA

In this era of apes, thinking is confined strictly to the here and now, with thinking solely focused on specific situations.

MIMETIC ERA

Then, humans communicated their thoughts by physically representing them. Learning was by imitation.

David Geary

THE ORIGIN OF MIND

BIOLOGICALLY PRIMARY KNOWLEDGE

Learning this type of knowledge is easy, natural and often unconscious. We are wired to learn it for reasons of survival, with the social skills of relating to others at the centre.

John Sweller

COGNITIVE LOAD THEORY

MEMORISED COGNITION

Sweller and colleagues built their theory on the long-term and working memory loop.

EMBODIED COGNITION

Paas and colleagues reported how gestures can augment WM capacity.

CHAPTER
FOUR COGNITIONS

SPREADS
01 WHY THIS BOOK? | 02 CRITIQUE & CONTROVERSY | 03 PHILOSOPHICAL ORIGINS |
04 METAPHORS | 05 COGNITIVE SCIENCE | 06 EVOLUTIONARY PSYCHOLOGY |
07 COGNITIVE LOAD THEORY | **08 INFOGRAPHIC SUMMARY**

 ### SITUATED COGNITIVE LOOP

 ### DISTRIBUTED COGNITIVE LOOP

Projecting thoughts and manipulating objects helps us think more effectively.

We think, learn and remember better through conversations with others.

CONNECTIONS

- A RESULT OF COGNITIVE SCIENCE DISCIPLINES' NEW IDEAS ABOUT THE MIND
- RELATES TO EVOLUTIONARY PSYCHOLOGY AND UPDATED CLT

 ### MYTHIC ERA

 ### THEORETIC ERA

Humans added gesture, then language to their repertoire, helping reconstruct the past and discuss the future.

Capturing ideas in writing and images greatly developed communal iterative thinking by making them permanent.

CONNECTIONS

- SKILLS FROM EARLIER ERAS ARE RETAINED AS FULLY FUNCTIONAL VESTIGES
- THEORETIC ERA COINCIDES WITH THE BIOLOGICAL SECONDARY PHASE

BIOLOGICALLY SECONDARY KNOWLEDGE

 Only relatively recently have humans gathered in groups to teach their children facts, concepts and skills not directly related to survival. So learning such content is not natural and requires effort and self-control. There are few concrete correlates to the concepts encountered.

CONNECTIONS

- BIOLOGICALLY PRIMARY LEARNING IS USED TO ACCOUNT FOR CLT NEW STUDIES
- SECONDARY KNOWLEDGE STARTED WITH THEORETIC ERA

SITUATED COGNITION
Van Merriënboer and colleagues identified how the environment is a causal factor in learning.

DISTRIBUTED COGNITION
Kirschner and colleagues recognised the phenomenon of group working memory.

CONNECTIONS

- CLT HAS HAD AN EVOLUTIONARY UPGRADE WITH THE INCLUSION OF THESE OTHER COGNITIONS
- THEY COINCIDE WITH THE EXTENDED MIND

EMBODIED COGNITION

SITUATED
COGNITIVE
LOOP

EMBODIED
COGNITIVE
LOOP

DISTRIBUTED
COGNITIVE
LOOP

WM

MEMORISED
COGNITIVE
LOOP

EMBODIED COGNITION OVERVIEW

I move, therefore I remember – physical movements, including gestures, have been shown to boost memory.

The hindrance of the solo mind

Annie Murphy Paul

> *The world is full of far more information than our conscious minds can process.*

MURPHY PAUL, A., 2021

Pawel Lewicki

NONCONSCIOUS INFORMATION ACQUISITION. THE HUMAN COGNITIVE SYSTEM IS NOT EQUIPPED TO HANDLE SUCH TASKS ON A COGNITIVELY CONTROLLED LEVEL

The sheer quantity of information available in any one given moment for us as humans to process is staggering. Our verbal and auditory cognitive processing capacities are limited but we have many more tools at our disposal. There are multiple ways in which we can utilise our bodies and harness the power of the processing connections between body and mind.

Interoception

We store and reference huge swathes of information on a nonconscious basis throughout each day, storing regularities of experience and identifying patterns on a subconscious level and in volumes our consciously controlled memory cannot handle. Yet, we draw on these stored patterns in our mental archives alongside our conscious active remembering. Our bodies will often then 'tip us off' with a physical response such as a sigh or a shiver or a tensed muscle. 'The body is rung like a bell to alert us to useful and otherwise inaccessible information.' We are all aware of and will have experienced these interoceptive capacities which have been referred to as our 'somatic rudder'. These subtle signals that there is more going on within our bodies than can be processed by our conscious minds is an illustration of one aspect of embodied cognition.

The movement effect

SEE **SPREAD 13** TO READ MORE ABOUT THE MOVEMENT EFFECT

The knowledge that movement is beneficial to health is widely understood and accepted, as is movement's positive effects on overall mood. What are less widely accepted are the positive effects of movement on cognition.

**EMBODIED
COGNITION**

CHAPTER

2

We know from Merlin Donald's work on the stages of the making of the modern mind that each evolutionary stage is preserved as a fully functional vestige. Humans becoming hunter-gatherers meant that from a previously relatively sedentary existence, there was now a duality and synchronicity of challenge between mind and body. We evolved to become thinkers on the move.

Our modern educational approach has championed the singular development of the mind alongside an equating of stillness with steadiness and industriousness during learning; all this to the exclusion of the mind's natural partner, the body.

The stillness effect

Langhanns and Müller's work on the effects on movement and cognitive load produced results which showed that a focus on self-regulation and stillness actually increased cognitive load significantly and reduced overall success in solving problems when subjects were asked to be still. The capacity to regulate attention, movement and behaviour is a limited resource and used up when suppressing or ignoring a natural urge to move.

What movement does is the opposite and it can have lasting effects. From the low intensity movements of simply standing or walking while working, to the long lasting beneficial effects of moderate exercise on attention, verbal fluency, cognitive flexibility, problem solving, decision making and increases in working memory, it is the mind on the move which has the greater power and potential.

Our classrooms are often still and sedentary spaces, with upwards of 50% of a young child's school day spent static and sitting. Alongside the benefits of both the effects of general movement and exercise, there are also the significant and specific effects of congruent, novel, self-referential and metaphorical movements in our teaching. Movement can ready us for learning and our bodies themselves can be highly successful tools for teaching and learning.

Merlin Donald

EACH COGNITIVE ADAPTATION IN HUMAN EVOLUTIONARY HISTORY HAS BEEN RETAINED AS A FULLY FUNCTIONAL VESTIGE.

Christine Langhanns & Hermann Müller

SUBJECTS' COGNITIVE LOAD CONSIDERABLY INCREASED UNDER THE INSTRUCTION NOT TO MOVE.

Pinja Jylänki

FUNDAMENTAL MOTOR SKILL AND PHYSICAL ACTIVITY INTERVENTIONS MAY SUPPORT COGNITIVE AND ACADEMIC SKILL LEARNING IN CHILDREN.

GESTURES

We are all effectively bilingual – fully fluent in gesture.
Gesturing improves understanding and boosts memory.

Annie Murphy Paul

🔳

GESTURES DON'T MERELY ECHO OR AMPLIFY SPOKEN LANGUAGE; THEY CARRY OUT COGNITIVE AND COMMUNICATIVE FUNCTIONS THAT LANGUAGE CAN'T TOUCH.

Gesture as the leader

In the process of learning, there will be points at which our fledgling understanding is hazy and inchoate. We are unable to find the exact words to convey our burgeoning ideas. We may not be able to find the words but our bodies are one step ahead – the leading edge of our thoughts. The use of gesture does not just serve to season our words with clarity or emphasis through simple beat gestures; gesture is both a window into understanding *and* a tool we can employ to secure understanding in others.

Gestural foreshadowing

Studies by Christian Heath involving hundreds of videoed explanations by multiple subjects have demonstrated how ideas show up in gesture before they appear in our words. In fact, on the cusp of understanding, it is our hands that hold the answers as to what is going on in our heads.

Susan Goldin-Meadow

🔳

LEARNERS WHO PRODUCE SUCH SPEECH-GESTURE MISMATCHES ARE ESPECIALLY RECEPTIVE TO INSTRUCTION – READY TO ABSORB AND APPLY THE CORRECT KNOWLEDGE, SHOULD A PARENT OR TEACHER SUPPLY IT.

We see this writ large from the development of early language too. Babies can point and gesture long before they can articulate their wants in coherent words. It is the same with more complex ideas. When we cannot find the words, it is our hands that do the talking. This use of our bodies to express an overview of a concept not yet fully formed or yet to be expressed is known as 'gestural foreshadowing'. If we want to know what our pupils know and understand, we need to observe what they say with their bodies as much as we see what they write or hear what they say.

As Goldin-Meadow's research shows us, gestures congruent with speech will show us mastered material; mismatched or diverged speech and gesture show us a transitional state where pupils are particularly receptive to instruction.

Beyond hand waving – spontaneous and designed gestures

Use of gesture alongside speech provides both an additional memory trace as well as lightening the cognitive burden and mental load by offloading an overreliance on the auditory onto our hands.

Some of our gesturing is spontaneous and in response to the natural articulation of intelligent thinking. However, designed gesture can be harnessed to enhance memory and understanding.

Designed gesture is particularly effective at reinforcing memory. This proprioceptive hook, the feel of our hands making a gesture reinforces our memory, even if we hide our hands from view when making the gesture.

By thinking carefully about the congruence between our spoken words and our gestures, and encouraging our pupils to use these designed gestures, we can also help to outline concepts which can be hard to capture in words alone and especially those which may be image rich or beyond direct perception such as the size of the universe or how tiny a single cell may be. Our bodies can give life and sense to concepts our words simply cannot convey effectively.

Integrating gesture

Gestures improve spatial thinking and advance our understanding of complex concepts, as well as reduce our cognitive load and improve our memory.

How we script and intentionally use gestures to accompany our explanations and how we then encourage our pupils to integrate these movements into their own gestural lexicon can have a huge impact. Gesture has the power to make the discrete and linear verbal explanation into a rich 3D understanding of complex concepts using our ancestral shared native language.

Spencer Kelly

HAND GESTURES APPEAR TO ALERT THE AUDITORY CORTEX THAT MEANINGFUL COMMUNICATION IS OCCURRING.

Manuela Macedonia

DESIGNED GESTURES CAN ACT AS AN AID TO MEMORY ... ENACTING A GESTURE WHILE LEARNING A WORD HELPS TO CEMENT THAT WORD IN MEMORY.

ON-SCREEN GESTURES

Small screen sizes and workspaces reduce our access to embodied resources and increase cognitive load.

Robert Ball

TURN AWAY FROM CHOOSING TECHNOLOGY THAT ITSELF IS EVER FASTER AND MORE POWERFUL, TOWARD TOOLS THAT MAKE BETTER USE OF OUR OWN HUMAN CAPACITIES – CAPACITIES THAT CONVENTIONAL TECHNOLOGIES OFTEN FAIL TO LEVERAGE.

Enhancing teaching by harnessing what we learned during remote learning

Due to the pandemic, schools are now well trained in the practical aspects of remote delivery. By merging what we know about these practical aspects with what we know about cognition, we can further enhance learning.

Larger workspaces result in more expansive thinking

The traditional use of multiple stacked windows on small screens does not allow you to harness the benefits of the embodied cognition loop. Much of the body's inbuilt functionality is wasted. By using larger or multiple screens, it is possible to utilise your embodied resources. Larger screens allow us to absorb more information through our peripheral vision and proprioception.

Larger workspaces reduce cognitive load

There is also a reduction in cognitive load as the data displays remain permanent and visual. When students use larger screens, they orientate their bodies to the content and record information as if the ideas were physical objects in physical spaces.

Robert Ball

EVERYONE WHO ENGAGES WITH A LARGER DISPLAY FINDS THEIR THINKING IS ENHANCED

The same benefits apply to non-digital workspaces

Obviously, in most classrooms, increasing screen sizes isn't a viable option. But as you will see on spread 17, there are many practical options for harnessing your students' embodied resources by using space as a resource.

SEE **SPREAD 17** TO READ MORE ABOUT USING SPACE AS A COGNITIVE RESOURCE

CHAPTER
EMBODIED COGNITION

SPREADS
09 EMBODIED COGNITION OVERVIEW | 10 GESTURES | **11 ON-SCREEN GESTURES** |
12 GESTURES & CHECK FOR UNDERSTANDING | 13 MOVEMENT | 14 BRAIN-BODY-WORLD
TOGETHER – NATHAN TAYLOR | 15 PLAN FOR GESTURING

EMBODIED
COGNITION

CHAPTER

2

Learning from videos

What can be seen during the use of video affects learning.
The positioning of the face and body and the use of gesture
all contribute to overall learning effectiveness. Richard E.
Mayer's *The Cambridge Handbook of Multimedia Learning*
says research shows having the speaker's face on during
online learning makes no difference. Also, research from
Yale University led by Joy Hirsch has recently revealed
through brain scanning that the social areas of the brain
which are activated when we learn from someone face to
face are absent when viewing a pre-recorded video.

In addition to the absence of specific brain activation,
pre-recorded videos don't provide opportunities for back-
and-forth conversation, the kind which is championed
by Professor Robin Alexander through dialogic teaching.
This process of responses from one person being linked
to another person's initiates the process of learning and is
known as contingent communication. Hirsch's research
showed when it was absent, learning may simply fail to
occur – a phenomenon known as 'video deficit'.

Joy Hirsch

*EYE CONTACT OPENS
THE GATE BETWEEN TWO
PERCEPTUAL SYSTEMS OF
TWO INDIVIDUALS, AND
INFORMATION FLOWS.*

On-screen gestures

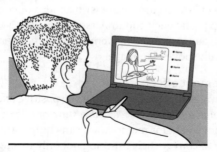

Annie Murphy Paul

*INSTRUCTIONAL VIDEOS
THAT INCLUDE GESTURE
PRODUCE SIGNIFICANTLY
MORE LEARNING FOR
THE PEOPLE WHO WATCH
THEM.*

Gesture supplies and supplements meaning for both the
teacher and the learner. Instructional videos which include
gesture produce significantly greater learning gains than
those where the speaker's hands are obscured. Teachers
need to ensure their hands are visible at all times while on
screen and to encourage students to gesture back.

GESTURES & CHECK FOR UNDERSTANDING

If gestures become more precise and refined with understanding, we ought to pay attention to the movement of our students.

Checking for understanding

Annie Murphy Paul

> *Gesture brings an uncertain future into the observable present. It imbues it with realness.*

MURPHY PAUL, A., 2021

When checking a learner's understanding, our focus is often on the words they say or on the written recording they produce. We infer the depth of their understanding and the points of their misconceptions by listening or reading. In the case of listening to answers, we use the words they say to infer how close to a version of correct they are. In the case of marking, this inference and analysis is often done after the event, far away from the learner themselves.

Barbara Tversky

AS OUR COMPREHENSION DEEPENS, OUR LANGUAGE BECOMES MORE PRECISE AND OUR MOVEMENTS MORE DEFINED.

Gestures offer another layer of evidence

Using what we know about gestures and movement, we can harness their power to enrich our inference about what learners are thinking and understanding. Gestures offer us *a profusion of extra-verbal meaning* which we need to be aware of and then ready to receive and interpret. It is also an indication of how secure we are with an idea or concept. As we develop proficiency and understanding with a concept or process, our associated movements become more precise just like with spoken language.

SEE **SPREAD 10** TO LEARN MORE ABOUT DESIGNED GESTURES

The movement effect

By combining what we know about the positive effects on memory of associating a *designed gesture* or one of the *four types* of movement for memory, we can equip learners with the ability to convey their thinking not only through their words but also through their movements.

1 2 3 4 5

CHAPTER
EMBODIED COGNITION

SPREADS
09 EMBODIED COGNITION OVERVIEW | 10 GESTURES | 11 ON-SCREEN GESTURES |
12 GESTURES & CHECK FOR UNDERSTANDING | 13 MOVEMENT | 14 BRAIN-BODY-WORLD
TOGETHER – NATHAN TAYLOR | 15 PLAN FOR GESTURING

Observe your students' gestures

By actively looking for evidence of these designed gestures
and deliberate movements during student explanations,
we can look for those learners who may be on the cusp
of understanding and most receptive to intervention and
instruction. These will be those learners who are struggling
to articulate their thinking in words but whose gestures are
rich with fledgling understanding.

↗
SEE **SPREAD 15** TO
LEARN HOW TO CREATE
OPPORTUNITIES
FOR GESTURE IN THE
CLASSROOM

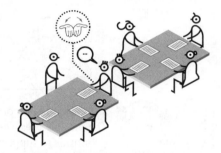

*The teacher demonstrates the concept.
When using words alone, the student's
answer lacks confidence and precision.*

*However, when the student uses the
same gestures as the teacher during
their explanation, they begin to show
early signs of understanding.*

Gestures allow for early intervention

Rehearsal of new vocabulary or concepts, when twinned
with a designed gesture or deliberate movement, provides
not only an additional memory trace for learners, but
also additional information for the teacher to check for
understanding. Just as listening for integration and accurate
use of new vocabulary can be used to infer understanding,
so too can deliberate observation of the learner's use of
gesture. The power of observed gesture, however, is that
intervention to support misconceptions and build on early
understanding can be actioned earlier in the learning
process compared to waiting for correct verbal or written
responses.

Susan Goldin-Meadow

🗩

*WHEN THERE'S A
MISMATCH BETWEEN
SPEECH AND GESTURE –
THEN THAT INDIVIDUAL
CAN BE SAID TO BE IN A
TRANSITIONAL STATE,
MOVING FROM THE
INCORRECT NOTION
SHE'S EXPRESSING IN
WORDS TO THE CORRECT
ONE SHE IS EXPRESSING
IN GESTURE.*

MOVEMENT

Moving can help boost comprehension and memory. No, this does not mean you should dance in your science lesson.

Helga & Tony Noice

ONE MIGHT PARAPHRASE DESCARTES AND SAY, 'I MOVE, THEREFORE I REMEMBER'

Our bodies act as translators

When we are learning our first nursery rhymes, packed with narrative and new vocabulary, these are often accompanied by actions: Incey Wincey Spider, Five Little Ducks, Wind the Bobbin Up. Our bodies act as translators and illuminators for the newly encountered words and their meanings.

> The incey wincey spider...

> went up the water spout...

> ... and washed the spider out

Helga & Tony Noice

MOVING MAKES AN ESSENTIAL CONTRIBUTION TO STRENGTHENING MEMORY

This association of a movement with new learning need not be the sole preserve of early language acquisition but can continue to supplement cognitive capacity throughout our lives. Outcomes of studies in young adults by the Noices on the strengthening effect on memory of integrating movement show:

- Information is better remembered when we're moving as we learn it.

- Movements need not be literal enactments of the information; they need only be meaningfully related.

- Information associated with movement is better remembered when we can reproduce that movement later when calling it up from memory.

Movement aids comprehension

A study by Beilock found that 'people who have moved in different ways go on to think in different ways' with the term 'facilitated comprehension' being used to describe the positive impact the integration of movement had on the speed at which subjects could process information.

CHAPTER
EMBODIED COGNITION

SPREADS
09 EMBODIED COGNITION OVERVIEW | 10 GESTURES | 11 ON-SCREEN GESTURES |
12 GESTURES & CHECK FOR UNDERSTANDING | **13 MOVEMENT** | 14 BRAIN-BODY-WORLD
TOGETHER – NATHAN TAYLOR | 15 PLAN FOR GESTURING

**EMBODIED
COGNITION**

CHAPTER

2

Four types of movement

Congruent movement
Using the body to enact the exact meaning, for example, physically moving along a number line.

Novel movement
Experiencing a new movement and feeling the physical effect to explain a previously unknown process.

Self-referential
Imagining being part of a process, for example, imagining you are particles during their changing state.

Metaphorical
Activation of a spatial metaphor such as 'on one hand/on the other hand'.

Movement gives memory a helping hand

When planning for memory, teachers can enhance cognitive capacity and recall by ensuring pupils are not *relegated to the role of observer* but instead ensure they are physically participative. By deliberately planning for specifically aligned movements with taught content, which are then practised each time the concept or vocabulary is revisited, teachers can harness the embodied cognition loop to strengthen that of the memorised cognition loop.

The repeated experience of the body moving in a specific way deliberately aligned with content allows the power and positive effects seen with the use of manipulatives to be transferred to that most ever available and flexible manipulative, the body. And these movements need not be large-scale gross movements with students up on their feet, but simple hand movements to demonstrate a process such as moving the arms to create the equals sign.

Sian Beilock

MOVING THE BODY CAN ALTER THE MIND BY UNCONSCIOUSLY PUTTING IDEAS IN OUR HEAD BEFORE WE ARE ABLE TO CONSCIOUSLY CONTEMPLATE THEM ON OUR OWN.

Nathan Taylor
JFK SPECIAL SCHOOL

Brain-Body-World together

The Extended Mind presents an alternative perspective of cognition to current theories for the teaching of children with profound multiple learning disabilities.

Profound provocations

Intrigued by the idea of thinking outside the brain drew me to Annie Murphy Paul's book about the extended mind. I was drawn to the principles set out in the conclusion that provoked an alternative perspective on cognition and learning for children with PMLD.

Children with profound and multiple learning disabilities (PMLD)

I work with children with PMLD, which is a definition that includes a severe intellectual impairment, physical disability, sensory impairment and/or a severe medical condition. Children with PMLD are often absent from debates in education or they are considered only as an afterthought. This is exemplified in national policy in changes to assessment, with statutory guidance only coming into force in September 2021.

Curriculum tensions

The Department for Education asserts that children with profound disabilities learn within a non-subject specific curriculum. However, a definition of a non-subject specific curriculum is absent. The very notion of an alternative challenges education professionals who believe the national curriculum is inclusive framework. This opens a space for debate about how children with PMLD develop their understanding.

Innate potential

Geary suggests cognition can be considered as biologically primary and biologically secondary abilities. To state simply, primary biological knowledge develops through experience – children's engagement in the world – due to innate capabilities humans have at birth. Secondary cognitive abilities are culturally specific and require specific teaching, for example, reading or mathematics. I suggest here that most children with PMLD learn within the biologically primary abilities throughout their lives.

CHAPTER
EMBODIED COGNITION

SPREADS
09 EMBODIED COGNITION OVERVIEW | 10 GESTURES | 11 ON-SCREEN GESTURES |
12 GESTURES & CHECK FOR UNDERSTANDING | 13 MOVEMENT | **14 BRAIN-BODY-WORLD
TOGETHER – NATHAN TAYLOR** | 15 PLAN FOR GESTURING

Engagement and enhancement

One criticism of Geary's biological primary knowledge is
that it is overly simplistic. This is fair when reflecting on
the teaching of children with learning disabilities, as they
require different levels of support than their able-bodied
peers. I propose combining the recognition of primary
knowledge with strategies to enable engagement enhances
learning potential. However, this may not be a simple cause-
to-effect correlation.

Not simply input and output

A reflective pedagogy is defined for the purposes of
understanding how children with PMLD learn. The role
of teacher-as-observer is to identify small variations in
performance by the child. Theoretically embedded in
behavioural psychology, notions of progress focus on
nuanced responses to stimuli stated as progression in small
steps. Andy Clark challenges causality presented in this way.
Influenced by phenomenologist, Maurice Merleau-Ponty,
Clark suggests a synergy he terms 'continuous reciprocal
causation'.

Taking the windy path

Annie Murphy Paul asks us to resist a computational
understanding of thinking. Engagement for children with
PMLD is not about stimulus response. Instead, it is like a
loop. Cognition is a dynamic process that is not situated in
the confines of the brain. For children with PMLD I argue
it requires what Mitchell J. Nathan terms a 'collaborative
embodiment'. Cognition, particularly for children with
PMLD, is socially contingent. Learning occurs through the
body and by working with other bodies. One prime example
of this is using body signs as a form of communication.
Body signs demonstrate how thinking goes beyond simple
stimulus response as meaning is derived not simply from
touch and action as it is also situated.

Annie Murphy Paul

*SOMETHING ABOUT
OUR BIOLOGICAL
INTELLIGENCE BENEFITS
FROM BEING ROTATED IN
AND OUT OF INTERNAL
AND EXTERNAL MODES
OF COGNITION, FROM
BEING PASSED AMONG
BRAIN, BODY AND
WORLD.*

Mitchell Nathan

*RESTRICTING STUDENTS'
MOVEMENTS AND
SOCIAL ENGAGEMENT
DOES MORE THAN
MERELY IMPEDE THEIR
CONNECTION TO WHAT
THEY ARE SUPPOSED TO
BE LEARNING.*

PLAN FOR GESTURING

Don't leave gesturing to chance – engineer opportunities to make gestures a part of your classroom routines.

Purpose of strategy

Gestures boost students' vocabulary, aid their learning and enhance their memory. This strategy can help you to embed gesturing into your classroom routines.

Context of strategy

Gestures are considered to have little-to-no working memory cost. Therefore, students should be encouraged to gesture in all phases and subjects.

1 Plan for gesturing

Explore opportunities for integrating authentic gestures into your explanations. For example, in maths, use a finger to trace angles. In geography and science, use your hands to demonstrate tectonic plate movement.

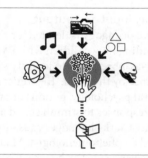

2 Model gesturing

While explaining a concept or process, use gestures that precisely capture your speech. Engineer opportunities for your students to practise these gestures. Use steps 3 and 4 to check for understanding.

3 Students use the gestures

Make sure all students use the gestures. Pair gestures with choral responses and direct students to use gestures during self and paired explanations. Use step 4 to check for gesture–speech matches.

CHAPTER
EMBODIED COGNITION

SPREADS
09 EMBODIED COGNITION OVERVIEW | 10 GESTURES | 11 ON-SCREEN GESTURES |
12 GESTURES & CHECK FOR UNDERSTANDING | 13 MOVEMENT | 14 BRAIN-BODY-WORLD
TOGETHER – NATHAN TAYLOR | **15 PLAN FOR GESTURING**

**EMBODIED
COGNITION**

CHAPTER

2

NOTES

Point 1
A gesture should capture what is being described with precision. Provide opportunities for students to practise gesturing and check their accuracy.

Point 2
Students are more likely to gesture when they have something to gesture at: pair gestures with objects and diagrams.

4 Check for understanding

While checking for understanding, don't just inspect students' verbal and written responses; make sure their gestures match their answers. The speech or writing should precisely describe the gesture. And vice versa.

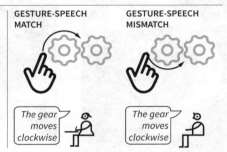

GESTURE-SPEECH MATCH

GESTURE-SPEECH MISMATCH

The gear moves clockwise

The gear moves clockwise

5 Gesturing during practice

During retrieval and independent practice, direct students to replay their explanations and gestures in their minds. This works especially well when recounting a diagram from memory.

One step at a time. A picture for every step.

https://youtu.be/
MInPwzg6TiQ

Fred Jones, once a teacher in a school for autism, in our favourite education video. Watch how he pairs gestures with choral responses.

45

SITUATED COGNITION

SITUATED
COGNITIVE
LOOP

EMBODIED
COGNITIVE
LOOP

DISTRIBUTED
COGNITIVE
LOOP

WM

MEMORISED
COGNITIVE
LOOP

SITUATED COGNITION OVERVIEW PT1

Experts are aware of the dangers of an overwhelmed mind; hence, their use of cognitive tools.

In *The Extended Mind,* Annie Murphy Paul explains situated cognition across three chapters: Thinking with Natural Spaces, Thinking with Built Spaces and Thinking with the Space of Ideas. For the purpose of this *In Action* book, we will focus on the chapter most applicable to classroom teachers: Thinking with the Space of Ideas.

Tools extend the limits of human cognition

Cognitive science is waking up to the idea that cognition doesn't reside solely in the brain; there is a growing agreement that it loops across the body and into the physical environment. Cognitive load theory now recognises the causal relationship between the physical environment and working memory. By physical environment, van Merriënboer et al. aren't just referring to the attributes of the built environment; they are also alluding to the physical characteristics of learning tools.

On spread 03, there are two illuminating examples of physical tools being used to extend human cognition. Both Richard Feynman and Otto use external tools to solve problems. In the classroom, teachers can include offloading devices to help students manage the limitations of their working memory. According to the research by van Merriënboer and colleagues, such devices give students' working memory a helping hand during cognitively demanding tasks.

Donald Norman

❯

THE POWER OF THE UNAIDED MIND IS HIGHLY OVERRATED. WITHOUT EXTERNAL AIDS, MEMORY, THOUGHT AND REASONING ARE ALL CONSTRAINED.

Jeroen van Merriënboer

... pencil, paper, pocket calculator, and white board can be used as off-loading devices when learners want to solve a problem easily or retain information longer.

CHOI, H.H., van MERRIENBOER, J. & PAAS. F., 2014

1 2 3

CHAPTER
SITUATED COGNITION

SPREADS
16 SITUATED COGNITION OVERVIEW PT1 | 17 SITUATED COGNITION OVERVIEW PT2 |
18 MANIPULATIVES | 19 MAPPING | 20 NOTE-TAKING – LEKHA SHARMA | 21 DRAWING FOR
LEARNING – ALISTAIR HAMILL | 22 TECHNOLOGY & THE EXTENDED MIND – RACHEL WHITE

External representations allow you to do more

In terms of their affordances, external representations
differ significantly from internal representations. External
representations allow humans to put distance between the
content of their minds and themselves. By doing so, they
benefit from what psychologist Daniel Reisberg calls the
detachment gain. The addition of space allows humans to
see their thinking and activate their powers of recognition.
You will be more familiar with the detachment gain
than you first might think. For example, when in doubt
about how to spell a word, you might write it out. Almost
immediately, you recognise if the spelling appears correct
or not. The correct spelling is locked up in your long-term
memory, but gaining access requires it to be externalised.

External representations reduce transience

The most profound leap in human cognition occurred
during what Merlin Donald calls, The Theoretic Era. This
stage of cognitive evolution is attributed to the ancient
Greeks who used written language to theorise. For the
first time, humans began using external representations
to capture their thoughts. In doing so, the ancient Greeks
produced what Charles Darwin called 'longer trains
of thought'. By capturing their speculative ideas, the
ancient Greeks could 'riff' on them and make incremental
refinements. External representations rescue our working
memory from the transient information effect.

External representations integrate cognitive loops

External representations allow students to augment their
thinking through multiple cognitive loops. For example,
students will be more likely to gesture when they have a
visual artefact to gesture at. Also, when students use a visual
artefact to explain to a peer, they divert working memory
resources to create narratives, free from the burden of
transient information.

THE TRANSIENT
INFORMATION EFFECT:
WHEN INFORMATION
DISAPPEARS BEFORE
IT CAN BE ADEQUATELY
PROCESSED, LEADING
TO INFERIOR
LEARNING THAN MORE
PERMANENT SOURCES
OF INFORMATION

Annie Murphy Paul

*PEOPLE ARE MORE
LIKELY TO GESTURE
WHEN THEY HAVE
SOMETHING TO GESTURE
AT. PROVIDING … VISUAL
ARTEFACTS – CHARTS,
DIAGRAMS, MAPS,
MODELS, PHOTOGRAPHS
– INDUCES SPEAKERS TO
GESTURE MORE.*

SITUATED COGNITION OVERVIEW PT2

The mind has a special relationship with the physical world; it is seen in our language and how we store memories.

Solving transience gave rise to a new problem

External representations in the form of written prose can reduce the transient nature of the spoken word. But marks (words and images) on paper or a screen have given rise to a new problem: poorly designed visual communication in a world containing a virtually unlimited amount of information. To navigate the seemingly endless amount of information in the world today, we draw on our prelinguistic experiences in physical spaces.

SPATIAL METAPHOR
EXAMPLES:
END IN SIGHT
NEXT STEPS
CENTRAL
PERIPHERY
GRASP IDEAS
PUT IDEAS ACROSS
ENCOUNTER
WIDEN POINTS OF
ACCESS

We all speak in spatial metaphors

Evidence from linguistics shows how our experiences in the physical world shape the way we think. You will find evidence of this in the language humans use every day. The work of linguist George Lakoff and philosopher Mark Johnson reveals how we use spatial metaphors to grasp abstract concepts. The metaphors studied by Lakoff and Johnson are not the literary decorations you might have learned in your English lessons. Instead, these are metaphors born out of our prelinguistic observations of the spatial properties of the physical world. Without these metaphors, it would be almost impossible to think or communicate any idea.

Kim Stachenfeld

OUR LANGUAGE IS RIDDLED WITH SPATIAL METAPHORS FOR REASONING, AND FOR MEMORY IN GENERAL.

We record memories in the same way we record places

Exciting developments in neuroscience are also revealing the relationship between the physical world and the way we think. Nobel prize-winning studies show that how we record where we have been parallels how we store memories.

In 1971, neuroscientist John O'Keefe discovered place cells in the hippocampus of rats. These place cells help rats remember where they have been. Four decades later, Norwegian neuroscientists May-Britt Moser and Edvard Moser (2010) discovered the more sophisticated grid cells in the nearby entorhinal cortex of the human brain. The growing consensus is that place and grid cells store information about space and time, recording locations and memories.

READ MORE ABOUT PLACE AND GRID CELLS: HTTPS://WWW. QUANTAMAGAZINE. ORG/THE-BRAIN- MAPS-OUT-IDEAS- AND-MEMORIES-LIKE- SPACES-20190114/

1 2 3

CHAPTER
SITUATED COGNITION

SPREADS
16 SITUATED COGNITION OVERVIEW PT1 | **17 SITUATED COGNITION OVERVIEW PT2** |
18 MANIPULATIVES | 19 MAPPING | 20 NOTE-TAKING – LEKHA SHARMA | 21 DRAWING FOR
LEARNING – ALISTAIR HAMILL | 22 TECHNOLOGY & THE EXTENDED MIND – RACHEL WHITE

External ideas are ripe for manipulation

Many disciplines – cognitive science, anthropology, linguistics and neuroscience – are pointing to an extended notion of cognition, whereby the physical world becomes an extension of the mind. These findings are why Barbara Tversky argues that 'the mind regards ideas as objects and when thought overwhelms the mind, the mind uses the world'. Annie Murphy Paul suggests that by putting our thoughts into the world, we can manipulate them, arrange them and see them anew. By doing so, we exploit space as a cognitive resource.

Space as a cognitive resource

Pulitzer Prize-winning author and historian Robert Caro is best known for writing voluminous political biographies. When planning his work, Caro offloads his thoughts onto a space large enough for physical navigation. Caro's office wall looks similar to the evidence walls you will have seen in most crime dramas. At a basic level, this space allows him to capture his thoughts. With his ideas offloaded, Caro's working memory is more likely to recognise any gaps in his thinking. Plus, he has more mental capacity to organise his work into a coherent structure.

Large workspaces make us efficient thinkers

Large workspaces, including oversized computer screens or multiple monitors, exploit our powers of spatial reasoning and memory. When using a large workspace, we can access information through our peripheral vision. Also, we can store more content in our minds as less cognitive bandwidth is used to find information. By using a large workspace, we relate the content to where it is located. We generate mental tags of the information's spatial location as we physically navigate the space in which it is held.

While it might not be possible to provide wall-size workspaces to our students, we can leverage their potential for spatial thinking by providing them with sticky notes, graphs, diagrams and graphic organisers.

Annie Murphy Paul

*... OFFLOADING
INFORMATION ONTO
A SPACE THAT'S
BIG ENOUGH FOR
US TO PHYSICALLY
NAVIGATE (WALL-SIZED
OUTLINES, OVERSIZED
CONCEPT MAPS,
MULTIPLE-MONITOR
WORKSTATIONS) ALLOW
US TO APPLY TO THAT
MATERIAL OUR POWERS
OF SPATIAL REASONING
AND SPATIAL MEMORY.*

MANIPULATIVES

Used in many fields of expertise – including science and architecture – manipulatives can assist complex thinking.

**Frédéric
Vallée-Tourangeau**

*THINKING WITH YOUR
BRAIN ALONE – LIKE A
COMPUTER DOES – IS
NOT EQUIVALENT TO
THINKING WITH YOUR
BRAIN, YOUR EYES AND
YOUR HANDS.*

MANIPULATIVES CAN
SUPPORT CONGRUENT
MOVEMENT. SEE
SPREAD 13 TO
LEARN MORE
ABOUT CONGRUENT
MOVEMENT.

Manipulatives can reveal what our students know

Our culture admires people who think in their heads. In contrast, many people perceive manipulatives as being childish, reserved for novices. But watch architects use models when planning large projects, and you will realise manipulatives are not just for children.

Experts use physical objects to reveal their thinking. Teachers can do the same to expose their students' thoughts and any misconceptions they might have.

Manipulatives can reveal what our students know

Manipulatives are not only a one way valve of moving from novice or concrete to expert and abstract thinking; they can also be used to bridge the truly abstract and make it concrete. Examples of this are the use of small world, role play and loose parts play resources alongside such staples as sand and water with young children.

Observing children acting out scenarios with these indefinitely imaginative manipulatives enables practitioners a window into the young children's worlds of social and emotional development as well as their understanding of science, maths and language.

Manipulatives simplify complex concepts

Manipulatives also provide dynamic and interrogative representations of challenging concepts.

Afshah Deen explains how she uses a number line to help students with telling the time. Initially using a physical number line drawn on card marked in intervals of fives to represent each block of five minutes, she then lifts the number line and twists to form a circle, effectively creating a clock face which demonstrates how the linear representation becomes circular. This allows a transference of the established concept of the linear representation to that of a circular one but maintains the ability to *undo* the circle and return to the familiar linear representation. Afshah also uses

1 2 3 4 5

CHAPTER
SITUATED COGNITION

SPREADS
16 SITUATED COGNITION OVERVIEW PT1 | 17 SITUATED COGNITION OVERVIEW PT2 |
18 MANIPULATIVES | 19 MAPPING | 20 NOTE-TAKING – LEKHA SHARMA | 21 DRAWING FOR
LEARNING – ALISTAIR HAMILL | 22 TECHNOLOGY & THE EXTENDED MIND – RACHEL WHITE

manipulatives to help bridge the stages of understanding in concepts such as the teaching of improper fractions and mixed numbers. By using numicon she can demonstrate – and pupils then explore – the relationships between the language, symbols and the concept by physically manipulating the numicon. The change in size and shape of the numicon for the different representations also has physical proprioceptive congruence with the concept.

Conceptual prototyping

By using manipulatives to pose questions and explore thinking, we can develop from a traditional master and apprentice simple *copy me* model of manipulative usage to an opportunity for exploring emerging thinking and concepts. By harnessing the ways in which *interactivity benefits performance* we can seek not only to reduce cognitive load by outsourcing our developing understanding to let the manipulatives do the heavy lifting, but we can construct a concrete conceptual prototype of emerging understanding which both learner and teacher can explore and interrogate.

NUMICON: BASED ON A PROVEN CONCRETE-PICTORIAL-ABSTRACT APPROACH, NUMICON ENCOURAGES CHILDREN TO EXPLORE MATHS USING STRUCTURED IMAGERY AND APPARATUS **OXFORD UNIVERSITY PRESS**

I gather all the vegetables I intend to use, and place them beside the sink. As each vegetable is washed I place it aside, separating it from the unwashed vegetables. When all are washed I transfer them to beside the cutting board, where I keep my knives, and begin chopping each in the way I will need it.

FROM
DAVID KIRSH'S
THE INTELLIGENT
USE OF SPACE

David Kirsh

THINKING WITH OBJECTS ENABLES FORMS OF THOUGHT THAT WOULD BE HARD IF NOT IMPOSSIBLE TO REACH OTHERWISE.

MAPPING

Mapping reveals meaning by revealing the underlying structure of knowledge.

Purpose of strategy

Mapping prevents content from being transient. At the same time, it exploits students' innate ability for spatial thinking and reasoning.

Context of strategy

Creating a stable artefact means students can engage in *longer trains of thought*. With their thoughts laid out, they can riff on them and see them anew.

---

1 | Select a graphic organiser

To show hierarchies or classifications, use a concept map. Compare information by using a Venn diagram. Present temporal information by using a flow chart and causal relations by using a fishbone diagram.

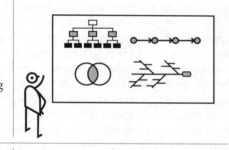

---

2 | Collect the ideas

Direct students to collect information from text or from memory if the mapping is for retrieval practice. Use sticky notes to capture each idea – one idea per note. Doing so will make it easier to arrange the content.

---

3 | Organise ideas

Group and rank ideas to show hierarchies. Compare by placing similar notions together and contrasting ideas apart; sequence ideas to show temporal events. And to depict causal relations, pair cause with effect.

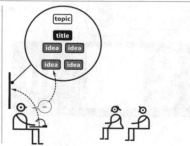

NOTES

Point 1
Each branch of the graphic organiser provides the perfect opportunity for *check for understanding*.

Point 2
Students should explain their diagrams and use gestures when they do.

4 Construct the organiser

Construct the organiser, piece by piece. Model the first stages of how to create the diagram. If the organiser is complex, or if a class is new to this strategy, use a template to scaffold its construction.

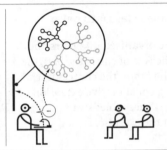

5 Refine and improve

Direct students to reconfigure sections of their diagram that don't stand up to common sense. Acknowledge when new iterations result in the discovery of new ideas. Peer explaining can assist this process.

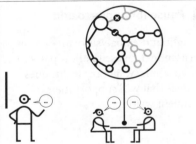

6 Use as a cognitive tool

Show how the diagram's structure can be exploited during extended writing. Have students use their organiser to explain their thinking to a peer. Teach students how to use it for self and peer quizzing.

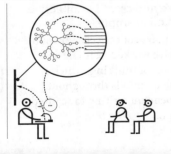

NOTE-TAKING IN PRIMARY WRITING LESSONS

Lekha Sharma explains how she uses note-taking in writing lessons to integrate cognitive loops and to reduce cognitive load during writing composition.

Lekha Sharma

THE JOHN WALLIS CofE ACADEMY

Purpose of strategy

To offer pupils the opportunity to shape their own external *writer's toolkits* during text analysis to draw on and consider when they go on to write.

Context of strategy

Lekha Sharma's approach to note-taking involves a structured approach that encourages her young writers to more independently develop their writing *voice*.

1 Organise class into pairs

Students are organised into pairs and are given the role of either the *pen* (the scribe) or the *brain* (the contributor) encouraging collaborative extension of cognition. These roles swap throughout the exercise.

2 Pause for pupils to add

Throughout the analysis of an excerpt of written text, pause to allow pairs to *bank* vocabulary, literary techniques and ideas that will support their subsequent writing.

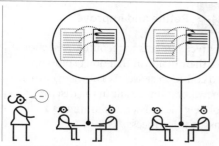

3 Share and create a collective worked example

As a class, pairs collectively contribute to a collective worked example of the collection of thinking, which is shared with all pupils throughout their independent writing to scaffold composition.

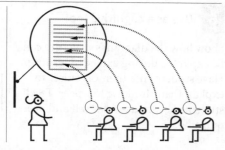

Purpose of note-taking for writing

By distilling a piece of text, students begin to recognise
the writer's decisions. Also, they augment their thinking
by creating an external artefact that they can use when
composing their own writing. By creating this situated
cognitive loop, students place their ideas and thinking to
one side, so to speak. The result: students' working memory
is less overwhelmed when engaging in writing.

Modelling note-taking for writing

Lekha believes that the process of pulling out the most
effective part of a writer's work needs to be modelled clearly
and uses the *think out loud* process to externalise why she
has chosen to add a particular tool to the toolkit. This is
something that she does orally during both reading and
writing lessons so students can begin to see reading and
writing as two sides of the same coin.

Checking for understanding

While pairs are discussing and capturing key tools from the
text, Lekha circulates the classroom and randomly pauses
the class to ask students to share what they have captured.
And most importantly, to justify why. The purpose of this
is twofold. 1) It reinforces the purpose of the task itself. 2)
It offers an additional scaffold for students who may be
struggling with the activity after the initial modelling of
this.

Modelling note-taking for writing

When students collectively share their responses, Lekha
encourages them to draw on one another's precis and
ideas to refine their own toolkits. She also asks students to
engage in activities to further augment thinking, such as
putting five selected writing techniques onto a sliding scale
dependent on how much of an impact they feel it will have
on the reader. This allows pupils to further develop their
choices and their own volition as writers.

DRAWING FOR LEARNING

How the act of diagram making can enhance the process of meaning making by students.

Alistair Hamill
LURGAN COLLEGE

Purpose of strategy

Getting the pupils to construct rather than just view diagrams requires the pupils to notice more, to select pertinent information better and to see how the parts relate to each other spatially as they make up the whole.

Context of strategy

Diagram construction with geography pupils.

1 Practice the basics

Using a visualiser, explicitly show how to move the arm, wrist and hand when drawing lines, arcs and curves. Practise this with pupils using warm-up exercises simply drawing these shapes repeatedly.

2 Identify constituent shapes

Show the pupils the constituent shapes you see in the final diagram (rectangles, arcs, lines) and draw them in the right position. Tracing paper can help scaffold this for them as they develop their skills.

3 Sketch, then ink

Graphic artists sketch lightly first to get the shapes right, then ink in definitive lines. Teach this workflow: light, fluid movements of the arm with a pencil, then ink more definitively with a pen.

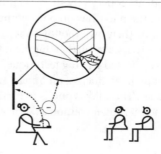

CHAPTER
SITUATED COGNITION

SPREADS
16 SITUATED COGNITION OVERVIEW PT1 | 17 SITUATED COGNITION OVERVIEW PT2 |
18 MANIPULATIVES | 19 MAPPING | 20 NOTE-TAKING – LEKHA SHARMA | **21 DRAWING FOR
LEARNING – ALISTAIR HAMILL** | 22 TECHNOLOGY & THE EXTENDED MIND – RACHEL WHITE

Once you have covered the basics of how to draw and given pupils a chance to practise towards automaticity, you begin to free up the cognitive space for them to access the affordances that diagram making can bring.

Bringing clarity to understanding and misconceptions

For a feature that exists in the real world, the shape, scale and placement of its elements matters. As my pupils draw diagrams, the *definiteness* of how and where exactly to form things on the page brings a clarity to their thinking, forcing them to think more precisely about those elements. It also helps me see any emerging misconceptions reflected in their drawings and clarify misunderstandings before they become embedded.

Encouraging interplay between drawing and thinking

Diagram construction can be more than simply copying pre-existing diagrams. Pupils can use their developing art skills to help them think generatively. For example, in one task, I gave my pupils a 3D cut away diagram of the tectonic context of the Himalaya region. I then asked them to produce a diagram rewinding time 50 million years to speculate on the tectonic scenario that preceded today's context. They had to imagine the scenario – and they had to *visualise* it. But what was fascinating to me was to see how these things were clearly happening concurrently for my pupils. The tentative sketching allowed them to externalise their ideas, making use of the affordance of *detachment gain*, the benefit that comes from being able to stand back a bit from our thinking. The pupils were moving away from a mindset that says, 'My diagram must be neat and perfect in its first form' to one that saw the visualisation as *part* of the iterative process of thinking and schema building.

It's as you see the image take shape on the page that you are better able to evaluate and reflect on your own thinking and meaning making. The affordance of definiteness brings clarity to thought otherwise difficult to achieve.

Annie Murphy Paul

TURNING MENTAL REPRESENTATIONS INTO SHAPES ON A PAGE SUPPORTED THE STUDENTS' GROWING UNDERSTANDING, HELPING THEM ELUCIDATE MORE FULLY WHAT THEY ALREADY KNEW

…AT THE SAME TIME, THE DEFINITENESS OF THE DRAWINGS THEY MADE REVEALED WITH RUTHLESS RIGOUR WHAT THE STUDENTS DID NOT YET UNDERSTAND, LEADING THEM TO FILL THE GAPS THUS EXPOSED.

TECHNOLOGY & THE EXTENDED MIND

How to use technology to enable all children in a classroom to access high-level content regardless of reading ability or proficiency in English.

Rachel White
BISHOP HENDERSON SCHOOL

Purpose of strategy

If all children are to access challenging material in lessons, some will require greater support than others. This strategy does this in a manageable and empowering way.

Context of strategy

By harnessing software designed to support reading and with one device per child, all children can access the same material independently.

---

1 Preparation

Using Microsoft Teams, assign all children to a team and create a Class Notebook within OneNote. Place all written materials in OneNote.
HINT: convert any PDFs to Word files.

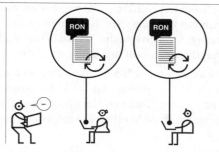

---

2 Activate Immersive Reader

Once children are working independently, they can use Immersive Reader (inbuilt in OneNote) to have the material reread to them or translated into their home language.

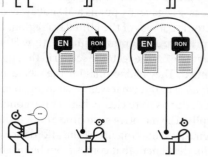

---

3 Revisit

Children can revisit the material at any time, are not limited by their ability to read or their understanding of English and access the same material as the rest of the class, independently.

Tools can help students become independent

Over the past two years, Bishop Henderson School has been researching the impact of having one laptop per child in Years 4–6. The intention is to widen access points to challenging material by using features built into Microsoft products. As a school, we want to boost students' independence by educating them to create cognitive loops between their working memory and situated technology.

Tools can mitigate the limitations of working memory

Immersive Reader is one such feature. The feature reads written text back to the students while highlighting words and removing unnecessary information. It also translates the content into the students' home language. Such features help students temporarily bypass the cognitive load imposed on them when encountering a second language. As such, students can get to the crux of the knowledge to be acquired.

Technology can extend students' minds

Ana joined Bishop Henderson School from Romania after a term in Scotland. In her previous school, she was taught Year 1 material due to her understanding of English. There was a concern that Ana was being excluded from her peers as she could not access the same material. The language barrier meant there was a mismatch between what Ana was being taught and her cognitive capabilities.

Starting at Bishop Henderson, Ana was instantly able to work on the same material as the rest of the class using Immersive Reader and Google Translate. Ana learned to successfully extend her mind, creating a situated cognitive loop to access the same challenging material as her peers. Ana gained confidence and friends and began to feel included. After one term of using these resources, her English has improved so much that she rarely uses them now. She is fully integrated into the class and achieving in line with her peers.

Mary Myatt

ALL CHILDREN SHOULD BE FOLLOWING THE SAME COURSE OF WORK, ENTITLED TO DO DIFFICULT THINGS AND SUPPORTED ON THE WAY. ALL CHILDREN ARE ENTITLED TO THE RICHNESS AND DIFFICULTY OF AUTHENTIC MATERIAL.

DISTRIBUTED COGNITION

SITUATED
COGNITIVE
LOOP

EMBODIED
COGNITIVE
LOOP

DISTRIBUTED
COGNITIVE
LOOP

WM

MEMORISED
COGNITIVE
LOOP

DISTRIBUTED COGNITION OVERVIEW PT1

Distributed cognition promotes inclusiveness, making us better thinkers as we learn to extend the mind by running our thoughts through others.

The hindrance of the solo mind

Annie Murphy Paul

> *We are inherently social creatures, and our thinking benefits from bringing other people into our train of thought.*

MURPHY PAUL, A., 2021

Today, solo-authored publications account for less than 10% of scientific journal articles and 25% of business articles. Scientists and economists know the limitations of cognitive individualism. They know solo thinking is insufficient to cope with the complexity and abundance of information in the world. To solve the most complex problems, experts create distributed cognitive loops. That is to say: experts run their thoughts through the minds of others.

Mitchell Nathan

SCHOOLS DO STUDENTS LITTLE SERVICE BY ARTIFICIALLY ISOLATING STUDENTS FROM THE SOCIAL AND ENVIRONMENTAL RESOURCES THEY NEED TO THINK, LEARN, AND CREATE.

Distributed cognition promotes inclusiveness

Providing students with opportunities to distribute their thoughts has many benefits. Arguably, none more significant than creating inclusive learning environments. For some young people, their socio-economic status dictates that they are very rarely listened to at home. Having someone interested in what they are thinking or what they have to say is unfamiliar to them. Teachers need to create situations that require group cooperation, helping students see the value in consulting and listening with their peers. Every student deserves to know their voice matters.

Distributed cognition makes us better thinkers

In *The Extended Mind*, Murphy Paul highlights many practical opportunities for humans to distribute their cognition. She reviews research demonstrating how imitating, debating, cooperating and teaching or being taught by peers helps make humans better thinkers. In subsequent spreads, we will show how teachers can assist students in creating distributed cognitive loops.

CHAPTER
DISTRIBUTED COGNITION

SPREADS
23 DISTRIBUTED COGNITION OVERVIEW PT1 | 24 DISTRIBUTED COGNITION OVERVIEW PT2 |
25 COGNITIVE APPRENTICESHIP – JOHN TOMSETT | 26 DOUG LEMOV'S STAR |
27 TEACHING WITH GROUP WORK – SAMMY KEMPNER | 28 PAIRED TEACHING

**DISTRIBUTED
COGNITION**

CHAPTER

4

Cognitive apprenticeship

Germany's economic dominance over the rest of Europe has lasted decades. Economists point to their extensive apprenticeship programmes as one of the country's main strengths. In *Cognitive Apprenticeship*, Collins et al. (1991) point out that apprenticeships make visible the thought processes of experts, whereas in traditional schooling, the thought processes are often invisible.

SEE **SPREAD 25**
TO LEARN MORE
ABOUT COGNITIVE
APPRENTICESHIP

Cognitive apprenticeship is a form of imitation

When experts make their thinking visible, they invite their students into cognitive loops whereby the best strategies to a problem are available. Consequently, students become more likely to replicate the thought processes of an expert. With this in mind, it seems uncontroversial to suggest cognitive apprenticeship is a form of imitating. You have already seen from Merlin Donald's work that mimicking was an adaptation in the evolutionary development of the modern mind. And developmental psychologists believe imitation causes infants to absorb so much information at a rapid rate.

Annie Murphy Paul

*IF WE ARE TO EXTEND
OUR THINKING WITH
OTHERS' EXPERTISE,
WE MUST FIND BETTER
WAYS OF EFFECTING AN
ACCURATE TRANSFER OF
KNOWLEDGE FROM ONE
MIND TO ANOTHER.*

Teachers can leverage the act of imitating to help their students acquire the knowledge they need. Plus imitating need not be considered mindless copying. In social science, the correspondence problem describes when someone adapts a solution and uses it to solve a new problem. If students are to crack the code, they must understand and articulate the solution, breaking it down into its individual parts, and reconfiguring it in new ways. When done well, imitating can demand a lot of students, requiring them to think hard.

SEE **SPREAD 27** TO
READ ABOUT WHAT THE
CORRESPONDENCE
PROBLEM LOOKS LIKE
IN SAMMY KEMPNER'S
CLASSROOM

DISTRIBUTED COGNITION OVERVIEW PT2

Humans have evolved to be social creatures. Teachers can tap into their students' burgeoning sociability in the service of learning.

Annie Murphy Paul

TEACHING IS A MODE OF SOCIAL INTERACTION WE CAN DELIBERATELY DEPLOY IN ORDER TO THINK MORE INTELLIGENTLY.

The teaching instinct

The act of teaching is present in every human culture around the world. According to archaeological evidence, humans have been teaching each other for hundreds of thousands of years. And there is evidence of teacher behaviour among toddlers as young as three and a half. As a species, we are sensitive to the cues of others – body language, eye contact and tone of voice. Humans have evolved into social creatures. In *The Extended Mind*, Murphy Paul recommends teachers leveraging this burgeoning sociability in the service of learning. With structure and under the right conditions, students can be used as a learning resource for one another, channelling their evolutionary instinct to teach.

It seems reckless to suggest using students to teach one another. But as you will see on subsequent spreads, opportunities do exist to distribute teaching in a way that ensures learning happens. Students as teachers works because it forces students to be metacognitive. While listening to a peer, students are monitoring the knowledge of both the speaker and themselves. Such a dynamic allows the actual teacher to listen to group interactions, holding students to account for individual and group success.

Confirmation bias

CONFIRMATION BIAS – INTENTIONALLY SELECTING AND BELIEVING EVIDENCE THAT SUPPORTS OUR EARLIER BELIEFS

Individual cognition is dangerously susceptible to confirmation bias. Humans don't need much incentive to scrutinise and evaluate the arguments of others but are less so inclined to examine their own. In *The Extended Mind*, Murphy Paul points to various studies which suggest active debate is the solution to confirmation bias.

During debates, humans make use of their inclination to evaluate the arguments of others. But more than that, rather than engaging in a sort of internal conversation, a debater can divide their thoughts among other debaters. Sharing propositions in this way relieves debaters of the burden of hosting internal debates in their heads.

DISTRIBUTED COGNITION

CHAPTER

4

The group mind

You'll recall reading on spread 07 that collaborative learning is more effective than individual learning when students encounter complex material. Despite its apparent benefits, many teachers appear reluctant to engage in group work. It is easy to see why; as Kirschner et al. (2018) point out, 'very little research actually moves beyond fuzzy feel-good explanations as to how and why group learning can be beneficial'.

When working in groups, students gain from each others' expertise. But as Murphy Paul explains, unstructured group work can be disastrous. For students to run their thoughts through the minds of their peers, there needs to be structure and a culture whereby they are motivated by collective success over individual goals. The following spreads contain practical strategies to assist teachers in the use of collaborative learning.

SEE **SPREAD 07** TO LEARN MORE ABOUT THE COLLECTIVE WORKING MEMORY EFFECT

> *...when groups work together on complex instructions they have a heightened level of confidence in their ability, as they are aware they can spread working memory load amongst other members of the group.*

KIRSCHNER, P. A., SWELLER, J., KIRSCHNER, F. & ZAMBRANO, J. R., 2018

Femke Kirschner

John Tomsett

EDUCATION CONSULTANT

Annie Murphy Paul

COLLINS NOTED A CRUCIAL DIFFERENCE BETWEEN TRADITIONAL APPRENTICESHIPS AND MODERN SCHOOLING: IN THE FORMER, 'LEARNERS CAN SEE THE PROCESSES OF WORK,' WHILE IN THE LATTER, 'THE PROCESSES OF THINKING ARE OFTEN INVISIBLE TO BOTH THE STUDENTS AND THE TEACHER.'

John Tomsett

TEACHERS MUST FIND A WAY TO APPLY 'APPRENTICESHIP METHODS TO LARGELY COGNITIVE SKILLS'.

COGNITIVE APPRENTICESHIP

Cognitive apprenticeship makes the implicit explicit by creating distributed cognitive loops between experts and novices.

The four dimensions of cognitive apprenticeship

In 'Cognitive Apprenticeship: Making Thinking Visible', published in 1991, Collins et al. took the traditional apprenticeship methods and applied them to schooling.

They focused particularly upon making the implicit, explicit, upon articulating aloud the unspoken. Because of the mass aspects of schooling, schools focus on teaching the explicit knowledge that has been accumulated in the textbooks and procedures that are taught in school. What is ignored is the tacit knowledge that adults acquire over a lifetime of solving problems and performing tasks.

The 'principles for designing cognitive apprenticeship environments' as conceived by Collins et al. are expressed within a framework consisting of four dimensions that constitute any learning environment: content, method, sequence, and sociology. The characteristics of each dimension are outlined below:

- **CONTENT: Types of knowledge required for expertise:** Domain knowledge, heuristics, control strategies, learning strategies.

- **METHOD: Ways to promote the development of expertise:** Modelling, scaffolding, coaching, articulation, reflection, exploration.

- **SEQUENCING: Keys to ordering learning activities:** Begin globally, increase in complexity, diversify.

- **SOCIOLOGY: Social characteristics of learning environments:** Situated learning, communities of practice, intrinsic motivation, exploit cooperation.

It would be easy for teachers to conclude that they are already using cognitive apprenticeship techniques in their classrooms. The question for teachers to answer is: 'How faithfully are you using the four dimensions of cognitive apprenticeship in your teaching?' If teachers tackle that question, along with the three posed opposite, they will have fuel aplenty to make disciplinary thinking visible.

CHAPTER
DISTRIBUTED COGNITION

Making teachers' expert thinking visible

For students to use the subject knowledge they possess, teachers must teach them what Collins et al. define as 'the usually tacit knowledge that underlies an expert's ability to make use of concepts, facts, and procedures as necessary to solve problems and carry out tasks'.

The teacher is the expert in the room. They have to provide opportunities for students to create distributed cognitive loops by seeing how an expert thinks. In so doing, the teacher expands their students' access to intellectual thinking. Also, students gain access to a larger pool of solutions to the problems they must solve.

Collins et al.'s 'Cognitive Apprenticeship' focused on reading, writing and mathematical problem solving. But cognitive apprenticeship can help define the expert thinking processes for each subject in the curriculum. All subjects and phases afford opportunities for students to offload their cognition, seeing how experts solve problems. All subjects and phases can harness their students' evolutionary capacity for imitation.

When it comes to identifying the unique expert thinking processes in individual subjects and different phases, those processes are rooted in domain knowledge.

Making subject teachers' expert thinking visible is key. In departments, they should consider three questions, which constitute a clear three-stage process to work through:

- How do you think like an expert (very specifically) in your subject discipline?

- How do you forge distributed cognitive loops with your students: making visible your expert subject disciplinary thinking?

- How do you teach your students to be expert subject disciplinary thinkers, helping them adopt the tacit knowledge you wish to impart?

Their answers will help make their expert thinking visible.

John Tomsett

🗩

USE COGNITIVE APPRENTICESHIP TO HELP DEFINE THE EXPERT THINKING PROCESSES FOR EACH SUBJECT IN THE CURRICULUM.

DOUG LEMOV'S STAR

If students are to reap the rewards of distributing their cognition, they are going to need some structure.

Gain from others' working memory capacity

In 'An Evolutionary Upgrade of Cognitive Load Theory', Paas and Sweller review cognitive load research into collaborative learning (distributed cognition). The findings of Paas and Sweller parallel those of Murphy Paul: in structured learning environments, students can benefit from the collective working memory effect. By distributing their cognition, students can gain from each other's working memory capacity. Some problems are too complex to be solved by a single mind. By distributing the effort, students working in a group share the burden of complex thinking. They tap into each other's working memory, creating a collective learning community.

We have evolved to learn from others

The inclusion of the collective working memory effect in cognitive load theory should come as no surprise. After all, humans have evolved to learn from others; we have an evolutionary advantage over other mammals. In TLAC 3.0, Lemov details how the cooperative eye hypothesis explains why humans have evolved to learn and think with each other. The sclera – the white outer portion of our eyes – allows humans to track each other's eye movement. Such an evolutionary adaptation is not seen anywhere else in the mammal kingdom. The result is humans are aware of the messages conveyed in their peers' eyes. By tracking the gaze of a peer, humans can tell if they belong to a group or not. We have physiologically evolved to cooperate with others because we depend on each other for survival.

Thinking with others requires structure

Unstructured group work is ineffective. But as Lemov shows in TLAC 3.0, highly organised collaborative learning can boost students' habits of attention and vice versa. To provide meaningful guidance to teachers on increasing students' habits of attention through group learning, Lemov uses the acronym STAR (shown right).

THE COLLECTIVE WORKING MEMORY EFFECT: COLLABORATIVE TASKS ALLOW GROUP MEMBERS TO GAIN FROM EACH OTHER'S WORKING MEMORY CAPACITY

SEE **SPREAD 06** TO LEARN MORE ABOUT THE EVOLUTION OF THE MODERN MIND

Annie Murphy Paul

I'M CONVINCED THAT WE NEED MORE STRUCTURED WAYS OF COMMUNICATING IF WE ARE TO 'THINK WITH' OTHER PEOPLE MORE EFFECTIVELY.

CHAPTER
DISTRIBUTED COGNITION

STAR is an intentional effort to distribute cognition

By developing attention habits through group work, teachers intentionally guide their students to distribute their cognition.

SIT UP — Instruct students to sit up when listening to their peers. A strong posture, and positive expression, shows students are in sync.

TRACK — To show students their voice matters, direct them to turn to face the student speaking. If the speaker sits at the front, have them turn to face the class.

APPRECIATE — Direct students to give off warm signals, such as nodding when a peer is speaking. By doing so, students gain a warm sense of acceptance.

REPHRASE — Have students rephrase the words of their peers, showing the speaker everyone was listening. Elaboration also re-exposes students to content.

Doug Lemov

... IT SEEKS TO USE THE SIGNALS PEOPLE SEND WHEN THEY ATTEND TO SOMEONE ELSE TO BUILD A STRONGER, MORE INCLUSIVE LEARNING COMMUNITY.

REPHRASING THEIR PEER'S WORDS RE-EXPOSES STUDENTS TO CONTENT, ALLOWING STUDENTS TO PRUNE ANY ERRORS WHILE BOOSTING THEIR MEMORY

Class, let's track Donald please.

APPRECIATE

REPHRASE

TEACHING WITH GROUP WORK

How does Sammy Kempner use group work – and avoid all the traditional mistakes – when teaching maths?

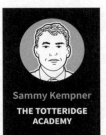

Sammy Kempner
THE TOTTERIDGE ACADEMY

Purpose of strategy
To make students intrinsically motivated for group success over individual goals.

Context of strategy
Sammy Kempner's approach to group work is highly structured. He sets challenging expectations and holds all students to account.

1 Set up the groups

Groups of three or four students work best as it is likely one of the students will know how to approach the question. Set up groups by matching high-attainers with low-attainers.

2 Teach each other

Have students teach each other by questioning, guiding and retesting each other. To show they have understood, students must make notes, in their own words, about the strategies required to answer each question.

3 Check group progress

Survey the class to identify students most likely not to know the answer. Ask the identified students what they have learned from their peers. If they can't articulate their thinking, hold the student's group to account.

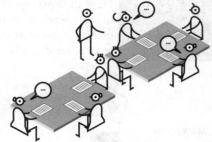

DISTRIBUTED COGNITION

CHAPTER

4

When to use group work

Group work should only be used when there is enough knowledge in the room. Kempner checks for this by using data from tests, mini whiteboards or circulating during independent practice. Kempner believes the two best times to use group work are during test reviews and guided practice.

Checking for understanding

When teaching each other, Kempner discourages his students from simply explaining a strategy or process. If they do explain, they must test their partner's understanding by making them explain it back to them. The teacher-students are encouraged to guide their peers through questioning and creating practice tasks. To further demonstrate what they learn, the taught-students make notes in their own words. Their recorded notes reveal whether or not they have understood the steps used to solve the problem. If they can't articulate the solution in their own words, they have not grasped it.

Making the group accountable

While student-teachers are questioning, guiding and retesting their peers, Kempner surveys the class, identifying students most likely not to know the answer. He asks the identified students what they know. If they can't articulate their thinking, the student's group is held accountable. If they can answer the question, Kempner will praise the group for their excellent teaching. The accountability in Kempner's classroom ensures students are motivated by group success over individual goals.

The ingredients needed for successful group work

If successful group work requires students to feel comfortable making errors, then students need training on how to teach each other, and established behaviour routines need to be in place. Frequently reminding students that making mistakes is a part of learning will boost their receptiveness to group work.

LISTEN TO SAMMY EXPLAIN TEACHING WITH GROUP WORK, ACCOUNTABILITY, AND CHANTS AT HTTPS:// WWW.OLLIELOVELL. COM/ERRR/ SAMMYKEMPNER/

Annie Murphy Paul

TEACHING IS A DEEPLY SOCIAL ACT, ONE THAT INITIATES A SET OF POWERFUL COGNITIVE, ATTENTIONAL, AND MOTIVATIONAL PROCESSES THAT HAVE THE EFFECT OF CHANGING THE WAY THE TEACHER THINKS.

SEE **SPREAD 24** TO LEARN MORE ABOUT THE TEACHING INSTINCT

USE SENTENCE AND QUESTION STEMS TO MAKE STUDENTS BETTER TEACHERS.

PAIRED TEACHING

Increase the frequency of feedback and student accuracy by activating students as a learning resource for each other.

DELIBERATE VOCABULARY DEVELOPMENT

Purpose and context

Investing in deliberate vocabulary development will widen your students' lexicon. Students will gain confidence and become more fluent at using complex vocabulary. Having students practise new words in pairs will also increase how much feedback both the students and teacher receive. It is as though there are 15 mini-lessons taking place at once.

1 Say the words aloud

Engineer opportunities for all students to say the words aloud. To check all students are saying the words, chorally, target individual rows, groups and pairs. This is useful when a word is difficult to pronounce.

2 Students rehearse

Provide opportunities for structured paired questioning, which forces students to use the to-be-learned words. The questions could include 'What does ... mean?' or 'Where else might you use this word?'

3 Check for accuracy

Circulate the room and monitor what students say to each other. As you survey the classroom, identify errors or misconceptions, and ensure discussions remain focused. Follow up by checking for understanding.

DISTRIBUTED COGNITION

CHAPTER

4

PAIRED RETRIEVAL

Purpose and context
Train your students to support each other in building confidence and fluency when retrieving knowledge. Using a knowledge organiser or equivalent resource, students can quiz each other and use elaborative questioning for retrieval practice. Again, both the students and teacher receive more frequent feedback.

1 Identify the knowledge

To ensure retrieval is meaningful, identify the knowledge you would like your students to rehearse. It is important that the quizzing helps students make connections, rather than simply remembering a list of facts.

2 Students quiz one another

To have your student provide expansive answers, model how to use elaborative questions, such as: how? Why? What? These sorts of questions explore processes, cause and effect, and making predictions.

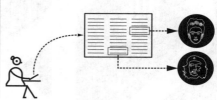

3 Check for accuracy

Circulate the room and monitor what students say to each other. As you survey the classroom, identify errors or misconceptions, and ensure discussions remain focused. Follow up by checking for understanding.

INTEGRATED COGNITION

SITUATED
COGNITIVE
LOOP

EMBODIED
COGNITIVE
LOOP

DISTRIBUTED
COGNITIVE
LOOP

MEMORISED
COGNITIVE
LOOP

INTEGRATED COGNITIONS

Intelligence, explains Murphy Paul, is '… a fluid interaction among our brains, our bodies, our spaces and our relationships.'

Understanding intelligence

Raymond Cattell

Forty years ago, Raymond Cattell distinguished two aspects of intelligence. One was termed 'fluid intelligence' and refers to the raw processing power we inherit from our parents. The other, 'crystallised intelligence', is the sum of the skills and knowledge we learn during our lifetime.

Changes in fluid intelligence and crystallised intelligence

Both intelligences are not static. Fluid intelligence rises then declines with age. Crystallised intelligence continues to rise as a result of our endeavours in encountering and learning about the world. This growth is in our hands.

HORN, DONALDSON & ENGSTROM 1980

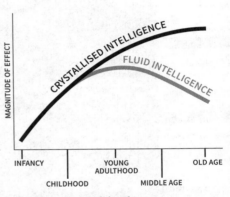

Crystallised intelligence and cognitive loops

If both the responsibility for and the control of growing crystallised intelligence lie with us, then it behoves us to exploit the potential of using all four cognitive loops for learning. Such a notion has started to change ideas about how to measure IQ. Andy Clark has recently started working with psychologists from the Netherlands on adapting the Raven's IQ test to measure the application of intelligence when 'extended with extra-neural resources'.

Annie Murphy Paul

The skilled use of extension is a proficiency that has gone largely unrecognised and uncultivated by our schools and workplaces, and it was long ignored by researchers in psychology, education and management.

MURPHY PAUL, A., 2021, P. 242

CHAPTER
INTEGRATED COGNITIONS

SPREADS
29 INTEGRATED COGNITIONS | 30 MAPPING MODE B WALKTHRUs | 31 THE EXMD IN FURTHER
EDUCATION PT1 – MARTINE ELLIS & VANESSA MEE | 32 THE EXMD IN FURTHER EDUCATION PT2
– SUE LAMBETH & DES GORMAN | 33 RECOUNT AND REDRAW

**DISTRIBUTED
COGNITION**

CHAPTER

5

Naming and the ontology of cognitive loops

In the absence of a shared vocabulary, much havoc – indeed,
damage – can often occur. In retrospect, it's now clear that
the prolonged, and continuing, distraction of learning styles
was aided by the lack of accurate naming and corresponding
research.

But, now, there is no such excuse. Since Chalmers and
Clark's paper on the extended mind, there has been
extensive research on cognitive loops and their significance
to the learning process. We can now adopt and integrate
this new nomenclature into our professional lexicon.

Equity of access to knowledge

At the end of her book, Annie Murphy Paul writes about
how we identify with our 'natural assets and abilities'
among which intelligence is paramount. Such a static – and
for many, disempowering – self-certification need not have
such a hold on development.

The potential of all four cognitive loops in enlarging
crystallised intelligence is enormous. It greatly increases the
points of access to knowledge for students.

In contemporary society, we now recognise and include a
wide range of differences among its members. Equity of
access to knowledge is of paramount importance to us.
Opening up points of access through the integration of the
cognitive loops available to students is an issue of equity.
This book is dedicated to that endeavour.

**Alexander
Grothendieck**

THIS GREAT
RUSSIAN–FRENCH
MATHEMATICIAN
EMPHASISED THE
POWER OF NAMING
IN ORDER TO GAIN
CONTROL OVER
OBJECTS – EVEN
BEFORE THEY'D BEEN
UNDERSTOOD

> *Defenders of the status quo have long argued that
> social and economic inequality merely reflects a
> kind of organic inequality, determined by nature, in
> the talents and abilities with which individuals are
> born. That argument appears less plausible when
> viewed through the lens of the extended mind.*

MURPHY PAUL, A., 2021, P. 252

Annie Murphy Paul

MAPPING MODE B WALKTHRUs

You'll recognise these cognitive loops in three Mode B strategies, as being familiar if not everyday.

Tom Sherrington

THE LEARNING RAINFOREST

Mode B emerges

Sherrington made teachers aware of Mode B thinking in his wonderful *The Learning Rainforest*, then later, in the two *WalkThru* books.

EMBODIED COGNITION

WALKTHRU 2

HANDS ON
—
Opportunities for first-hand experiences

SITUATED COGNITION

WALKTHRU 2

MUSEUM / GALLERY VISITS
—
Maximising the value of trips beyond the classroom

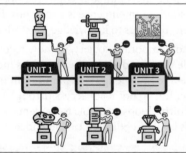

DISTRIBUTED COGNITION

WALKTHRU 1

ORACY: TALK FOR WRITING
—
Oral rehearsal as a precursor for writing

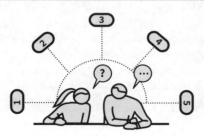

| 1 | 2 | 3 | | 5 |

CHAPTER
INTEGRATED COGNITIONS

SPREADS
29 INTEGRATED COGNITIONS | **30 MAPPING MODE B WALKTHRUs** | 31 THE EXMD IN FURTHER EDUCATION PT1 – MARTINE ELLIS & VANESSA MEE | 32 THE EXMD IN FURTHER EDUCATION PT2 – SUE LAMBETH & DES GORMAN | 33 RECOUNT AND REDRAW

DISTRIBUTED COGNITION

CHAPTER

5

The detailing of Mode B

When Tom wrote the Mode B WalkThrus, he didn't have the notions of *The Extended Mind* in his own mind. But we argue that it's possible to reinterpret them in terms of cognitive loops – and to see them in a new light. Here are three such examples.

Situated cognition | Direct encounters with objects

Doing is powerful. Holding objects, manipulating them – even changing them – provides information that is difficult, if not impossible, through words alone. Not only do students get new perspectives on the objects, the different views and the sensory input combine to form easily formed memories. Added to which is the conversation between peers that is naturally triggered. Cognitive loops, then, between sight, sensation and conversation.

Tom Sherrington

NUMEROUS ELEMENTS OF A GREAT KNOWLEDGE-RICH CURRICULUM REQUIRE STUDENTS TO GAIN KNOWLEDGE FIRST-HAND, THROUGH HANDS-ON EXPERIENCE.

Situated cognition | Seeing the past in concrete form

Physical spaces affect us. Think of how you respond to being in a cathedral, atop a mountain, at a museum. Walking from room to room, following a theme, envelops us in a novel sense of knowledge. Seeing the past represented in 3D, at scale, helps create physical and emotional sensations that are very potent. Concepts come alive. More than the intellect is affected. For some, lives are changed through new interests – even life trajectories.

Distributed cognition | Using others to develop ideas

Humans are social animals. Children and adolescents particularly so. That innate need to communicate can be harnessed to help students rehearse what they intend to write. Also, a conversation can help students move beyond a natural reaction to defend one's point of view. Feedback from a peer – spoken in a non-teacherly way – can trigger reflection and correction. Learning has an innate social dimension that can be effectively mobilised.

Martine Ellis

GUERNSEY COLLEGE

THE EXMD IN FURTHER EDUCATION PT1

We have a unique opportunity to embrace the concept of extended mind in FE due to the practical nature of what we do.

Martine Ellis, professional development manager at The Guernsey Institute explains:

Reflecting on my own professional practice, I assumed I must be far more *brainbound* than *extended* in my approach to thinking. I'm an avid reader and compulsive note-taker who spends a great deal of time in their head.

Getting intentional about extending the mind

Of course, it turns out I extend my mind all the time. When I am reading research or learning something new, I write about it on my iPad – *my second brain* – to develop my thinking. When I need creative ideas, I go for a walk. When I have a problem to solve, I talk it through with trusted colleagues or members of my online professional learning community. I use situated, embodied and distributed cognition every day.

Labelling these thinking approaches explicitly helps us use them more intentionally – both in terms of how we think (particularly in relation to our professional development) and how we support our students' thinking.

FE teaches students to marshal their extra-neural resources

We have a unique opportunity to embrace the concept of extended mind in FE due to the practical nature of what we do. Thinking, doing and collaborating are at the heart of our practice. While schools promote a brainbound approach, FE prepares students for the working world, where they must marshal extra-neural resources – extending their thinking – to thrive.

In this section, three of my colleagues share their interpretations of the extended mind in practice. Vanessa, a lecturer in education and training, presents three strategies for exploring embodied cognition with students. Des, a lecturer in engineering, explains his approach to distributed cognition through classroom debate. And Sue, a programme leader for students with SEND, shares her working wall concept as a practical example of situated cognition.

1 2 3 5

CHAPTER
INTEGRATED COGNITIONS

SPREADS
29 INTEGRATED COGNITIONS | 30 MAPPING MODE B WALKTHRUs | **31 THE EXMD IN FURTHER EDUCATION PT1 – MARTINE ELLIS & VANESSA MEE** | 32 THE EXMD IN FURTHER EDUCATION PT2 – SUE LAMBETH & DES GORMAN | 33 RECOUNT AND REDRAW

Vanessa Mee
GUERNSEY COLLEGE

EMBODIED COGNITION: THINKING ON YOUR FEET

Purpose and context

Get out of your head and into the moment: elevate the role physical engagement plays in cognition. Animate learners to trigger better learning.

Introduce opportunities in the classroom for movement to reinforce understanding, improve focus, problem solving and communication, and reduce cognitive load.

1 Heart on your sleeve

Teach learners how to tune in and respond to feelings, sensations and insights held within the body. Present the emotional landscape of the topic, acknowledge and explore responses.

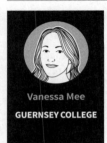

2 Act it out

Curate dynamic activities that spark active participation such as enacting meaning or metaphors, embodying objects and physicalising concepts. Allow learners to experience ideas in a concrete way through movement.

3 Talk to the hand

Enrich your verbal communication with symbolic gestures that imbue, imply and encourage meaning. Use air diagrams and hand punctuation to express beyond words. Devise a silent glossary and rehearse its delivery.

THE EXMD IN FURTHER EDUCATION PT2

Experts seamlessly extend their cognition across multiple cognitive loops. FE provides many opportunities to teach young people how.

Sue Lambeth
GUERNSEY COLLEGE

SITUATED COGNITION: THE WORKING WALL

Purpose and context

Create an offloading device to help students to manage the limitations of their working memory. Offloading frees up space for problem solving and exploring concepts.

Instead of using wall spaces for static displays that become invisible over time, use them as an oversized offloading device to develop thinking and ideas.

1   Clear the clutter

Clear the clutter in the room. Minimise distractions and fixed displays – these can be ignored and therefore unseen to the learner. This space can then be replaced with usable working space.

2   Create space

Create a space to extend thinking and give learners the *device* to offload information. The working wall can be used to explore topics, plan assignment work or to manage a group project.

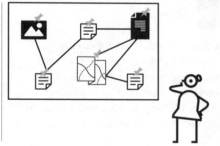

3   Work on the wall

When all of the information is on the wall, use it to direct discussion and encourage students to add and move items as needed. This oversized space optimises available capacity for thinking and exploring.

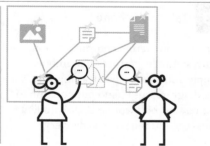

**DISTRIBUTED
COGNITION**

CHAPTER

5

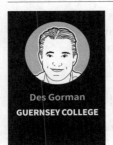

Des Gorman
GUERNSEY COLLEGE

DISTRIBUTED COGNITION: DEBATE IT

Purpose and context

Use group debate for complex topics. Distributing task chunks reduces cognitive load and enables students to share and connect their findings to improve understanding. In the engineering context a debate topic could be nuclear vs. fossil fuels as energy providers. Students engage in research, debate and critical reflection.

1 Research

Split students into groups. Appoint group leaders. Split the task up into chunks with individual students researching a particular element. Groups meet at least once during this stage to discuss ideas and strategies.

2 Debate

Stage the structured debate. Groups take it in turns to discuss their ideas and challenge each other's discussions. Hold a Q&A at the end to explore the topics in more depth.

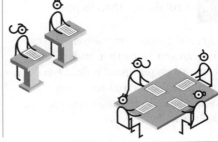

3 Review and reflect

Review the debate. Discuss collectively key points on both sides. Encourage understanding around opposing points of view. Set a summary task such as an article or presentation covering all elements of the concept.

RECOUNT AND REDRAW

Recount and Redraw assists students to spread their thinking across all four cognitive loops.

Purpose of strategy

Like a successful apprenticeship programme, this strategy reveals how experts think and organise knowledge. Students learn to *marshal and apply extra-neural resources.*

Context of strategy

Students create a visual artefact, helping them to gesture and explain their thinking to a peer. Plus, they'll boost their memory by recounting their diagrams unassisted.

1   Construct and explain the map

Draw a graphic organiser a branch at a time. As you construct it, explain your thinking. When the branch, or part, of the diagram is complete, direct your students to copy it.

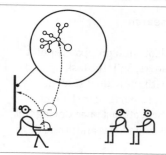

2   Explain the map to peer

Direct students to explain their diagrams to each other. Insist each keyword on the visual is defined with a minimum of two full sentences. Pairs swap roles; the explainer becomes the listener and vice versa.

3   Continue and complete

Continue to explain the content, its underlying structure and how it is arranged spatially in the diagram. Repeat steps two and three: students copy each branch and explain it back to a peer until the diagram is complete.

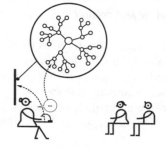

CHAPTER
INTEGRATED COGNITIONS

SPREADS
29 INTEGRATED COGNITIONS | 30 MAPPING MODE B WALKTHRUs | 31 THE EXMD IN FURTHER
EDUCATION PT1 – MARTINE ELLIS & VANESSA MEE | 32 THE EXMD IN FURTHER EDUCATION PT2
– SUE LAMBETH & DES GORMAN | **33 RECOUNT AND REDRAW**

DISTRIBUTED COGNITION

CHAPTER

5

NOTES

Point 1
Unsure which graphic organiser to use?
Visit https://www.organiseideas.com/work-1/posters
for support.

Point 2
Concerned your diagram is too complex? Why not create a
template to scaffold its construction?

4 Recount the whole map to peer

As students recount the whole visual
to a peer, direct them to trace the lines
of the diagram with their index finger.
When complete, the pairs switch roles.
Direct the listeners to ask interrogative
questions.

5 Redraw the map from memory

Ensure all copies of the map are out of
view. Direct the students to work alone
and redraw the map from memory.
Suggest they attempt to replay their
explanations and finger tracing in their
minds.

*Both gesturing and object manipulation may
be very old, very well-developed skills that are
acquired easily and can be used with a minimal
working memory load.*

John Sweller

PAAS, A. & SWELLER, J., 2012

REFERENCES

Abbott, A. (2021), THINK OUTSIDE THE BRAIN BOX: CAN OUR BODIES, TOOLS AND SURROUNDINGS TAKE MORE OF THE COGNITIVE LOAD?, Nature, 596: 181-182

Anderson, S. P. & Fast, K. (2020), FIGURE IT OUT: GETTING FROM INFORMATION TO UNDERSTANDING, Two Waves Books, New York, US
——

Ball, R. & North, C. (2007), REALIZING EMBODIED INTERACTION FOR VISUAL ANALYTICS THROUGH LARGE DISPLAYS, Computers & Graphics, 31: 380-400
——

Beilock, S. et al. (2008), SPORTS EXPERIENCE CHANGES THE NEURAL PROCESSING OF ACTION LANGUAGE, Proceedings of the Natural Academy of Sciences, 105: 13269-13273
——

Cattell, R. B. (1963), THEORY OF FLUID AND CRYSTALLIZED INTELLIGENCE: A CRITICAL EXPERIMENT, Journal of Educational Psychology, 54(1), 1-22
——

Choi, H. H., Van Merriënboer J. J. & Paas, F. (2014), EFFECTS OF THE PHYSICAL ENVIRONMENT ON COGNITIVE LOAD AND LEARNING: TOWARDS A NEW MODEL OF COGNITIVE LOAD, Educational Psychology Review, 26(2): 225-244
——

Clark, A. (2019), EXTENDED YOU, TEDxLambeth, https://www.youtube.com/watch?v=hanv8y_wYEQ
——

Clark, A. (2008), SUPERSIZING THE MIND: EMBODIMENT, ACTION AND COGNITIVE EXTENSION, Oxford University Press, Oxford, UK
——

Clark, A. & Chalmers, D. J. (1998), THE EXTENDED MIND, Analysis, 58 (1): 7-19
——

Claxton, G. (2015), INTELLIGENCE IN THE FLESH: WHY YOUR MIND NEEDS YOUR BODY MUCH MORE THAN IT THINKS, Yale University Press, London, UK
——

Collins, A., Brown, J. S. & Holum, A. (1991), COGNITIVE APPRENTICESHIP: MAKING THINKING VISIBLE. American Educator, 15(3): 6-11, 38-39
——

Descartes, R. & Cottingham, J. (1986), MEDITATIONS ON FIRST PHILOSOPHY: WITH SELECTIONS FROM THE OBJECTIONS AND REPLIES, Cambridge University Press, quoted in Foundations of Embodied Learning (Nathan, M. J.), 2022, Routledge, Abingdon, UK, p.14
——

Donald, M. (1991), ORIGINS OF THE MODERN MIND, Harvard University Press, Harvard, US
——

Dylan, B. (1964), WITH GOD ON OUR SIDE, The Times They Are A-Changin'
——

Geary, D. C. (2005), THE ORIGIN OF MIND: EVOLUTION OF BRAIN, COGNITION, AND GENERAL INTELLIGENCE, American Psychological Association, Washington, DC, US
——

Gibson, J. J. (1979), THE ECOLOGICAL APPROACH TO VISUAL PERCEPTION, Houghton Mifflin Harcourt, Boston, US

Goldin-Meadow, S. (2003), HEARING GESTURE: HOW OUR HANDS HELP US THINK, The Belknap Press of Harvard University Press, London, UK

Grothendieck, A. (2009), THE POWER OF NAMES: RELIGION & MATHEMATICS, PHILOCTETES CENTER, http://philoctetes.org/news/the_power_of_names_religion_mathematics

Heidegger, Martin (1927), BEING AND TIME (TRANSLATED BY JOHN MACQUARRIE & EDWARD ROBINSON), 1962, Blackwell, Oxford, UK, p. 99

Heyes, C. (2018), COGNITIVE GADGETS: THE CULTURAL EVOLUTION OF THINKING, The Belknap Press of Harvard University Press, London, UK

Hirsch, J. (2019), LOOKING DIRECTLY IN THE EYES ENGAGES REGIONS OF THE SOCIAL BRAIN, https://www.spectrumnews.org

Horn, J. L., Donaldson, G. & Engstrom, R. (1980), APPREHENSION, MEMORY, AND FLUID INTELLIGENCE DECLINE IN ADULTHOOD, Research on Aging, 3(1): 33-84

Jay Gould, S. (1985), THE FLAMINGO'S SMILE: REFLECTIONS IN NATURAL HISTORY, Norton, New York, US

Johnson, M. (1987), THE BODY IN THE MIND, The University of Chicago Press, Chicago, US

Jones, F. H. (2009), CREATING EFFECTIVE LESSONS THE EASY WAY WITH DR FRED JONES (VIDEO), https://youtu.be/MInPwzg6TiQ

Jylänki, P., Mbay, T., Hakkarainen, A., Sääkslahti, A. & Aunio, P. (2022), THE EFFECTS OF MOTOR SKILL AND PHYSICAL ACTIVITY INTERVENTIONS ON PRESCHOOLERS' COGNITIVE AND ACADEMIC SKILLS: A SYSTEMATIC REVIEW, Preventive Medicine, 155: 1-10

Kelly, S. (2012), THE BRAIN DISTINGUISHES BETWEEN GESTURE AND ACTION IN THE CONTEXT OF PROCESSING SPEECH, paper presented at the 163rd Acoustical Society of America Meeting, May 2012

Kempner, S. (2021), ERRR #056. SAMMY KEMPNER ON TEACHING WITH GROUP WORK, ACCOUNTABILITY, AND CHANTS (Podcast), https://www.ollielovell.com/errr/sammykempner/

Kirschner, P. A., Ayres, P. & Chandler, P. (2011), CONTEMPORARY COGNITIVE LOAD THEORY RESEARCH: THE GOOD, THE BAD AND THE UGLY. Computers in Human Behavior, 27(1): 99-105

Kirschner, P. A., Sweller, J., Kirschner, F. & Zambrano, J. R. (2018), FROM COGNITIVE LOAD THEORY TO COLLABORATIVE COGNITIVE LOAD THEORY, International Journal of Computer-Supported Collaborative Learning, 13: 213-233

Kirsh, D. (1995), THE INTELLIGENT USE OF SPACE, Artificial Intelligence, 73(1-2): 31-68

REFERENCES

Lakoff, G. & Johnson, M. (1999), PHILOSOPHY IN THE FLESH, Basic Books, New York, US, p. 397
___

Langhanns, C. & Müller, H. (2018), EFFECTS OF TRYING 'NOT TO MOVE' INSTRUCTION ON CORTICAL LOAD AND CONCURRENT COGNITIVE PERFORMANCE, Psychological Research 82(1): 167-176
___

Lemov, D. (2021), AMAZON BOOK REVIEW OF THE EXTENDED MIND
___

Lemov, D. (2021), TEACH LIKE A CHAMPION 3.0: 63 TECHNIQUES THAT PUT STUDENTS ON THE PATH TO COLLEGE, Jossey-Bass, San Francisco, US
___

Lewicki, P., Hill, T., Czyzewska, M., (1992), NONCONSCIOUS ACQUISITION OF INFORMATION, American Psychologist, 47: 796-801
___

Macedonia, M. (2013), LEARNING A SECOND LANGUAGE NATURALLY: THE VOICE MOVEMENT ICON APPROACH, Journal of Educational and Developmental Psychology, 3: 102-116
___

Mandler, J. M. & Cánovas, C. P. (2014), ON DEFINING IMAGE SCHEMAS, Language and Cognition, 6(4): 510-532
___

Miller, G. A. (2003), THE COGNITIVE REVOLUTION: A HISTORICAL PERSPECTIVE, Trends in Cognitive Sciences 7(3): 141-144
___

Moser, M-B. (2021), MAY-BRITT MOSER – FACTS, NobelPrize.org, www.nobelprize.org/prizes/medicine/2014/may-britt-moser/facts
___

Murphy Paul, A. (2013), BEYOND LEARNING STYLES, https://www.creativitypost.com/article/beyond_learning_styles
___

Murphy Paul, A. (2021), THE EXTENDED MIND: THE POWER OF THINKING OUTSIDE THE BRAIN, HMH Books, Boston, US
___

Murphy Paul, A. (2021), TWITTER 27.09.21, https://twitter.com/anniemurphypaul/status/1442262815838900233?s=20
___

Myatt, M. (2020), BACK ON TRACK: FEWER THINGS, GREATER DEPTH, John Catt Educational Ltd, Woodbridge, UK
___

Nathan, M. J. (2022), FOUNDATIONS OF EMBODIED LEARNING: A PARADIGM FOR EDUCATION, Routledge, Abingdon, UK
___

Noice, H. & Noice, T. (2006), WHAT STUDIES OF ACTORS AND ACTING CAN TELL US ABOUT MEMORY AND COGNITIVE FUNCTIONING, Current Directions in Psychological Science, 15: 14-18
___

Norman, D. A. (1993), THINGS THAT MAKE US SMART: DEFENDING HUMAN ATTRIBUTES IN THE AGE OF THE MACHINE, Reading, Mass, Addison-Wesley Pub. Co

Paas, F. & Sweller, J. (2012), AN EVOLUTIONARY UPGRADE OF COGNITIVE LOAD THEORY: USING THE HUMAN MOTOR SYSTEM AND COLLABORATION TO SUPPORT THE LEARNING OF COMPLEX COGNITIVE TASKS, Educational Psychology Review, 24, 27-45

Paivio, A. (1990), MENTAL REPRESENTATIONS: A DUAL CODING APPROACH, Oxford University Press, Oxford, UK, p. 55

Pinker, S. (2005), BOOK REVIEW OF THE ORIGIN OF MIND: EVOLUTION OF BRAIN, COGNITION, AND GENERAL INTELLIGENCE

Rowlands, M. (2013), THE NEW SCIENCE OF MIND: FROM EXTENDED MIND TO EMBODIED PHENOMENOLOGY, A Bradford Book, The MIT Press, London, UK

Shapiro, L. (ed) (2014), THE ROUTLEDGE HANDBOOK OF EMBODIED COGNITION, Routledge, Abingdon, UK.

Sherrington, T. (2020), THE LEARNING RAINFOREST: GREAT TEACHING IN REAL CLASSROOMS, John Catt Educational Ltd, Woodbridge, UK

Sherrington, T. & Caviglioli, O. (2020), TEACHING WALKTHRUS, John Catt Educational Ltd, Woodbridge, UK

Sims, S. (2021), EDUCATION ENDOWMENT FOUNDATION EFFECTIVE PROFESSIONAL DEVELOPMENT: GUIDANCE REPORT, EEF, London, UK

Stachenfeld, K. (2019), QUOTED IN CEPELEWICZ, J., THE BRAIN MAPS OUT IDEAS AND MEMORIES LIKE SPACES, QUANTA, www.quantamagazine.org/the-brain-maps-out-ideas-and-memories-like-spaces-20190114

Syed, M. (2019), REBEL IDEAS, John Murray, London, UK

Tindall-Ford, S., Agostinho, S. & Sweller, J. (eds) (2020), ADVANCES IN COGNITIVE LOAD THEORY, Routledge, Abingdon, UK

Tomsett, J. (2021), COLLINS ET AL'S COGNITIVE APPRENTICESHIP IN ACTION, John Catt Educational Ltd, Woodbridge, UK

Turkle, S. (ed) (2007), EVOCATIVE OBJECTS: THINGS WE THINK WITH, The MIT Press, London, UK

Tversky, B. (2019), MIND IN MOTION: HOW ACTION SHAPES THOUGHT, Basic Books, New York, US

Vallée-Tourangeau, G. & Vallée-Tourangeau, F. (2016), WHY THE BEST PROBLEM-SOLVERS THINK WITH THEIR HANDS, AS WELL AS THEIR HEADS, https://theconversation.com/why-the-best-problem-solvers-think-with-their-hands-as-well-as-their-heads-68360

Willingham, D. (2021), AMAZON BOOK REVIEW OF THE EXTENDED MIND